Landmark
BOOKS

D0922941

WILLIAM
THE
CONQUEROR

WILLIAM
THE
CONQUEROR

Thomas B. Costain

ILLUSTRATED BY
JACK COGGINS

Random House · New York

This is the story of a boy who was made the ruler of a warlike country when he was eight years old and who managed to compel obedience from the rebellious barons who surrounded him; who grew up to be a wise leader and an able general and who, moreover, had such great physical strength that no other man could bend his hunting bow; who envied a green and bountiful island and made war on the people who lived there with the result that a famous battle was fought. This boy who became one of the most turbulent figures of the Middle Ages was to be known ever after as William the Conqueror.

CONTENTS

WILLIAM
THE
CONQUEROR

CHAPTER I

A KING CHOOSES AN HEIR

William, the young son of Robert the Devil, Duke of Normandy, stood in the tapestry-covered archway, waiting for his father to summon him into the Great Hall. He could hear what his father was saying above the movement of mailed feet on the stone floor and the whispers of the assembled barons. He may have been thinking of his hunting dogs or of his favorite gerfalcon but he knew what was going to happen and he was both excited and glad. Every boy dreams of being a king, of sitting in judgment while all the adults kneel humbly in front of him; and young William of the strong back and sturdy limbs was going to have that privilege.

In the Great Hall, his father was addressing his clergy and lords upon a matter of extreme importance to the duchy. All eyes were upon him as he spoke. He was a commanding figure in his costly robes of state, his ermine mantle with golden clasp and glittering jewels. He was also called Robert the Magnificent because of his love of splendor, and, since he was holding a Great Council on that day, he wore his jewel-decked crown with the fleur-de-lys and held a drawn sword in his hand.

There was an air of suspense in the Great Hall as the Duke's words of welcome rang out. The Norman barons had come to his court in Fécamp, in the year of 1035, from their castles in every part of Normandy, bound in allegiance to answer his summons. As liegemen they expected that this might be another call to follow their lord into war; or perhaps a plea from the East to join the ranks of some king or prince in order to fight paganism. This would be to their taste, for the Normans were always ready to fight or to roam.

"My lords," said Robert, "I must make a grave decision at this time. I ask you to help me choose an heir!"

A hush fell over the gathering, and then a murmur rippled throughout the Great Hall. That their duke was concerned about an heir—he was barely twenty-four years old and in good health—came to them as a complete surprise. As he continued, their surprise changed to concern.

"Before the moon has waned," he went on, his eyes moving from face to face intently, "I shall have set out upon the road to the Far East to make a pilgrimage to the Holy City. God willing and with the help of the saints, I, a humble and contrite pilgrim, shall kneel before the Holy Sepulchre!"

A strong voice spoke up from the rear of the hall.

"My lord duke, many who set out for the Holy City do not return!"

The words spoken slowly were full of foreboding; a low murmur spread throughout the hall and out of it came a chorus of protests.

"It is a treacherous journey, my lord duke, even for a holy pilgrimage——"

"The hardships are great, sir duke, and every foot of the way is beset with thieves and evil spirits and murderers!"

Again the Duke motioned them to silence.

"By God and the resurrection," his voice rang out firmly, "I shall kneel at the Holy Sepulchre!"

Young William was peering through the tapestries. It seemed that all the barons, dressed in their most costly attire, were pressing toward the ducal throne where his father was seated. The scene was charged with excitement. His father alone seemed calm. He faced the dark and anxious countenances of his lords with quiet determination.

"It is folly, my lord duke," an excited voice cried. "Why submit yourself to danger and death? By our Lady, give up this pledge for the sake of Normandy!"

A stormy session followed this appeal to Robert. Every baron in the Council was seized with foreboding at the thought of his departure. They knew that once their leader had started on his pilgrimage

chaos would break out in the kingdom. Every ambitious Norman baron would immediately ride out
from his castle with his men-at-arms and pounce
upon his rivals, and even his neighbor, in order to
seize more land and power.

"For the sake of Normandy, stay, sir duke!"
other voices joined in the cry.

Finally Robert rose to his feet and held up both
hands to quiet the assembly. "I have sworn to go!"
he said with finality. "But you are wrong if you
think that I shall leave you without a duke of the
Normans!"

He turned toward the archway and beckoned. An attendant prodded the boy's shoulder but he might have spared himself the effort. Young William had already parted the tapestry and stepped out into the Hall. The barons fell silent at the sight of him and a tense air took possession of them. This was something they had not expected. Knowing the arrogant temper of Robert the Devil, they still had not thought him capable of this.

The silence remained unbroken as the boy made his way to the dais where his father sat. He was not frightened. Following instructions, he knelt before his father and then stood up and ranged himself beside the duke, his head held high, his eyes looking straight into the sea of faces before him.

"This is my son William," intoned the Duke. "Named for his grandsire, William Longsword, and sixth in direct line from Rollo, our illustrious ancestor. My lords, I give William my son to you."

A murmur spread through the gathering. Young William gazed upon the barons and when he saw their darkened faces and their frowns, he too began to frown, his dark eyes quite unabashed.

Finally the hush was broken by a quietly restrained voice.

"We beg of you, sire—give up your pilgrimage!"

The barons were not only perturbed but greatly embarrassed. Their duke had put them in a very difficult position. A boy ruler was the last thing they wanted when the country was seething with strife and lawlessness. Then, many of the older Norman barons, those of true Viking blood, were insulted that Robert the Devil should ask them to accept the boy William, son of a woman sometimes called Arletta, who was the daughter of the tanner of Falaise. Robert had rid himself of his real wife because she had borne him no children, and had then fallen in love with the handsome Arletta. He had set up an establishment for her, and had even brought her to the castle, but he had not married her.

The Duke looked about him and waved a haughty hand for silence.

"My lords," he cried, "I command you to take my son William to be your lawful ruler. I do hereby declare him my rightful heir. To him I leave all that I possess and to him I commend the kingdom of the Norman people."

Young William took his place before his father and, as he had been instructed, held out his hands, palms facing each other.

Now all eyes were fixed upon the boy, this sturdy boy with bright eyes and raven-black hair, square-faced, with his jaw as firmly set as his father's.

Slowly a war-scarred baron came forward from the assembly. He was from one of the more loyal districts of Normandy and one of Robert's faithful liegemen. The aging warrior knelt before the boy and placed his hands between William's. The words of his oath rang out firmly and convincingly. As he rose to his feet his place was taken by another baron. And so they came one by one, men with grave and troubled faces. They all knelt before the boy and swore that they would serve him faithfully; but there were many among them whose faces were dark and hostile, whose words sounded hollow, and whose eyes did not meet those of Robert the Devil, Duke of the Normans.

As the ceremony continued, a shadow fell over the assembly. The sun had been veiled momentarily by a dark cloud in the blue Norman sky, shutting out the light that streamed in the high windows of the Great Hall. To those present it was a sign, an ill-omen, that the boy William who might some day rule the "pirate land" of the Normans would be plagued with evil.

CHAPTER II

THE FIRST DUKE
OF NORMANDY

In order to understand the story of this remarkable boy William, it is necessary to know about the Norman people. They came from Norway and they were perhaps the fiercest of all the Vikings who set sail from that land to establish themselves on more hospitable soil. Certainly they were the most successful.

Rollo the Ganger, William's ancestor and the famous sea-king of the Northmen, was the first Duke of the Normans. He was so named because his legs were so long that he could not ride the small horses of his native land of Norway; he was forced to walk while others rode. Rollo called himself a sea-king and he had every right to do so. In those days any adventurer who sailed from the north was known as a Viking, but only one with royal blood could proclaim himself a sea-king.

In the tenth century, this huge and vigorous adventurer got into a dispute with the King of Norway, known as Harold-of-the-Beautiful-Hair, and was banished from the country. However, there were many Northmen who were only too eager to follow such a colorful leader as Rollo the Ganger in their search for adventure and desire to find some distant land where they might be free and prosperous.

When word spread that Rollo planned to set out with a fleet of Viking ships men clamored to go along with him. There were plenty of rogues who knew that it was wise to leave the country, as well as men who could not resist sailing away into unknown water, and soldiers who knew that such an expedition meant plenty of fighting and plundering.

There were also Northmen who were pioneers at heart and they felt sure Rollo would lead them to a fine land where they could settle.

The Normans knew how to build good sound vessels. They were known as dragon ships, and were fearsome-looking craft, rearing high both in bow and stern, with dragon figureheads and gilded tails that towered over the steersmen at the vessels' stern. The billowing sails were often of wide vivid stripes, and the vessels gleamed in the sunlight from the reflection of the sun on the silver shields that were slung over the sides. Sometimes these dragon ships were over a hundred feet long, with row after row of benches where the Northmen pulled at the oars.

The Vikings had to be hardy and daring. There were no holds below deck and the men slept out in the open. They sailed without charts or compasses, and the helmsmen had nothing but the stars to rely on in setting their course. Sometimes they carried baskets of ravens which they let go, so that they could follow their course and hope to reach shore.

There were gruesome tales of these men with the yellow beards who came in the dragon ships. When people saw the Viking sails come over the horizon (the soldiers came in the long-ships, followed by their cargo in the last-ships), they were terrified and fell on their knees fervently praying, "O good Lord, deliver us from the fury of the Northmen!" The sound of the ivory horns of the invaders was a warning to them to flee for their lives.

The Northmen plundered coastal areas of England on the east and Flanders on the Continent, working down to the channel districts of France. The French fought these plunderers but the King of France was powerless against Rollo and his Vikings. They swooped down upon the land around the mouth of the Seine River and even captured Rouen, one of France's greatest cities. The Vikings had come to stay and were willing to fight in order to do so. They were also quite ready to marry the French women and settle down. Very soon the Normans were giving up their own language and customs for those of the French. Before long these adventurers began to weary of war, as did the French. Rollo the sea-king was popular with his people and he had proved that he could govern as well as lead his men in adventure and battle. It seemed the opportune time for a truce.

In this way Rollo the Ganger became the first Duke of the new duchy of Normandy. He bowed before the King of France, placing his hands within the King's as he promised to serve him, to become his 'man.' He was given the King's daughter for a wife (at least there is such a legend), and he and his Vikings were baptized in the Christian faith. So the leader of the pirates became a vassal of France. The Northmen were now to be known as *Normans*.

Changes began to take place under Rollo's rule. Vikings who fought with him were given the very best tracts of land in the country and they became rich *seigneurs,* or feudal lords. Rollo, who had plundered like a pirate-king, now tried to rule his people with justice and order. He developed a means of protection for his kingdom that was unique with the Normans and which they were later to introduce to the English countryside. He built towering castles throughout Normandy, even in the depths of isolated forests. His men lived in these castles like lords. They were equipped and ready to fight for Rollo upon a moment's notice.

This new race of men with French and Viking blood were vigorous men who reveled in battle. They were clean-shaven with long noses and wore metal protectors on their helmets as if they specially valued their Norman noses. They could be recognized in battle by their kite-shaped shields, their scale armor, their conical helmets, and heavy two-handed swords. When they fought they rushed into action shouting *Dieu aide!* calling upon God instead of their pagan god Thor.

A hundred and twenty-five years later when Robert the Devil, fifth son of Rollo, ruled as duke of the Normans, his subjects were still pirates at heart. Endless bloody feuds raged on and on between the noblemen, for might was what counted in Normandy. They killed and maimed and took hostages, set fire to fields and forests, stormed enemy castles, and seized as much land as possible. The powerful lord was the one who could defend the most land and control the most land workers. The poor baron who could not muster enough soldiers to protect his castle was forced to fight under the banner of a stronger man, serving as his liegeman.

Robert the Devil tried to be a just and able ruler in the midst of this strife. He had the welfare of his people at heart, and they grew to respect him as well as fear him. But he was unable to stamp out the lawlessness and feudal wars. Too much pirate blood still flowed in the veins of his barons.

The situation became so bad that a man would not dare to walk down a deserted road in daylight with a sack of grain for fear of being robbed and murdered. Finally a *Truce of God* was called. This lasted from sundown on a Wednesday until the following Monday, and it was the only way that men could go about their work and survive. If anyone broke this truce he was subject to thirty years of hard labor. Unfortunately men took this time of truce to plan and plot for the days when they could strike for their own base ends.

Such were the Normans. They were not only great fighting men but they were also cool-headed, calculating, and acquisitive. They were as much at ease in a court of law as in the saddle, as willing to take over new possessions by crafty maneuvers as by force of arms. A strange combination, these Normans; a mixture of daring and guile, of courage and treachery; a winning combination, certainly.

The story of their seizure of land in northern

France and their conquest of England is one of the best known pages in history. Their greatest and most romantic exploit, however, is not as well known. It happened before Robert the Devil became Duke of Normandy. Two sons of Tancred of Hauteville, one of the Norman barons, set out for Italy in search of adventure. These two young men, Robert and Roger, not only conquered the southern provinces of Italy but crossed over and took the mountainous island of Sicily as well, thus setting up a great kingdom in the very heart of the Mediterranean. They were remarkable young men "of the greatest beauty, of lofty stature, of graceful shape—pleasant and merry, strong and brave, and furious in battle." The Normans of Sicily played a great part later in the Crusades.

CHAPTER III

WILLIAM'S BOYHOOD

When the council called by Robert the Devil had come to an end, the barons who reluctantly bowed before his iron will and pledged their allegiance to William rode home grimly, with drawn swords and in full armor, as if they expected immediate bloodshed.

Robert the Devil was well pleased with the outcome of his Council. He lost no time in carrying out the rest of his plans. He took the boy William to the court of King Henry of France where they were given a brilliant welcome. William now became the ward of King Henry. His cousin Alain, Duke of Brittany, was appointed the Regent of Normandy and he too knelt before their overlord, France's King. This was another strong bond between France and the one-time pirate land of Normandy.

Robert was now free to carry out his own journey. He set out barefoot, wearing the coarse cloth of a pilgrim and carrying a rude staff. The band of pilgrims accompanying him was a large one. He carried many costly presents in his train, and gave instructions that the horses were to be shod with silver shoes held in place by only one nail. As the silver shoes fell off by the roadside they were to be left in the dust, a generous gift of a devout and lavish pilgrim.

Robert the Devil did not return from his journey to the Holy Land. On the way home, within the year, he fell ill. Some believed that he was poisoned. He had to be carried by litter as the pilgrims made their way back to Normandy, and, as his barons had feared, death claimed him before the journey was over.

Thus the boy William became the ruler of Normandy, and from the moment that he was proclaimed the Duke of the Normans in his own right, his life was in constant danger. In fact, before he had grown to manhood he so narrowly escaped death time after time that it seemed his life was as charmed as the proverbial cat with its nine lives.

William had kinsmen who thought that they had a more legitimate right to rule Normandy. His

guardians and tutors did all that they could to protect him, but even they vied with each other for power. William's enemies resorted to murder in order to do away with three of them. As a child, the young Duke was continually being snatched out of danger and rushed to some place of safety.

One night as he slept in the strong castle of Vaudreuil, a murderer entered the keep and slipped by the attendants into William's chamber. Although it was dark he could see the outline of the sleeping boy in the large bed and he plunged a dagger into him. It happened that a boy companion was asleep beside the young Duke and it was he who was stabbed. In the confusion that followed, William was snatched away from the bed by his uncle. He clung to his rescuer and was taken to a place of hiding in the cottage of a loyal peasant.

His life was full of suspense and danger. Even so, William had to learn to rule his kingdom while he was still a youth. Before long stories began to spread throughout Normandy about his cleverness, his strength for his age, and what a born leader he was

—this baseborn boy whose grandfather was a humble tanner!

Like other Norman boys, William was greatly interested in two things—the chase and fighting. He had his own horse, a fleet-footed light Spanish horse that he could ride like the wind. He trained his own falcon, curving his arm so that the bird with its fettered claws sat upon his wrist proudly and rode with him. He was passionately fond of his dogs— the darting spaniels who were trained for bird hunts, and the terriers who liked to root out rabbits from their holes. He looked forward to the day when his kennels would have huge mastiffs so that he could go boar hunting, gazehounds that could outrun the prey on level stretches, and bloodhounds and slow-hounds for forcing animals out of their lairs.

The statement that no other man could bend William's bow has been made so often that it has become an accepted legend. If true, it was a proof not only of his great strength of arm but also of a special quality in the bows he used. The two great types had not come into use in William's time. The cross-bow became later the great weapon of the European archer. It was short, generally made of horn which was so stiff and strong that it could be bent only by turning a handle. Sometimes monster crossbows would be kept on the battlements of castles and these were of such a size and strength that they could be bent only by a windlass.

The longbow seems to have been used almost exclusively in England and Wales, and the Welsh are generally credited with having originated it. It was as long as the tallest yeoman and could send an arrow hurtling away almost out of sight. Lacking the terrific drive of the arrow propelled from the tight crossbow, it was nevertheless much the better and more deadly weapon. An English archer could loose three or four bolts from a longbow in the time that a Continental archer could wind up his crossbow for a single shot. It was the deadly rain of bolts from the longbow which won the great battles of Crécy, Poictiers and Agincourt.

In William's time there was only the short-bow. It was about half the length of the long one and

was accordingly much less deadly. It was made of yew or blackthorn, although sometimes on the Continent other woods were resorted to—the alder, the ash, the oak or the sallow. It is possible that, for the use of this muscular young ruler, an especially stout stave might be cut from the bole of a tree, so that the reddish grain of the yew would bend only at the command of a mighty arm. This much is certain: William's companions in the chase talked continuously about the straight line and the fury of the bolts he loosed from his bow and the way they transfixed the prey.

Reference has already been made to his love of hawking and his pleasure in carrying a gerfalcon on his wrist. The right to own a gerfalcon was confined to royalty and the varieties which other men could own was strictly according to rank. An earl, for instance, could have a peregrine, and a yeoman a goshawk, while servants were never allowed to have anything but a kestrel which was a very poor sort of bird indeed. All of these varieties were dark-eyed hawks, the powerful and deadly falcons of the North.

Learning to fight was a part of the boyhood of every young Norman, be he king's son or cook's son. By the time William was in his middle teens he could used a sword, a lance, and a mace with skill and ease. His shoulders had broadened, his limbs were lithe and strong. He could even wield the great two-handed sword like a true descendant of Rollo.

Of course he had to study in order to become a ruler, but this did not faze William. He learned logic, geography, and arithmetic, taking them all in his stride, and could even explain Caesar's *Commentaries* when he was still a boy. Once he was heard to say, "An ignorant king is no better than a crowned ass!"

William could beat all his friends at dice games and chess and dart-throwing. Whenever they played at war, he was the leader, commanding mock troops and giving orders from the throne. When there were fights and disputes, William was singled out to settle them, and he was unusually fair and honest with the others.

CHAPTER IV

AT THE FRENCH KING'S COURT

Being a ward of Henry, the King of France, William had to spend some years at the French court. He was well-built, tall and strong for his age, and long before his other companions were ready to do so, William was riding and taking part in the exercises for games of war. His ambition at this time was to ride his own rearing, plunging battle horse and to wear the golden spurs of a knight.

Meanwhile in Normandy, the barons were battling each other for more power, and Raoul de Vace, who was William's new guardian and friend, went to the King of France to ask that William be sent home to Normandy to rule his people.

Finally the day that William had been waiting for came!

It was a clear sunny day with plenty of crispness in the air. It seemed that all of Paris had turned out to take part as best they could in the festival and ceremony at the King's court. It was the day that the young noblemen of France and her vassals were to become knights. The market places had been filled to overflowing for many days with musicians and tradesmen laden with enticing wares. Visitors were flocking into the city to eat and drink and spend their money as they waited for the morning of the big day when the ceremony of knighthood would take place.

There were celebrations in Normandy on this day too, for William was one of those who were to receive the golden spurs of knighthood and the loyal Normans were proud of him. They were also thankful that he was proving to have the characteristics of a leader. They were only too ready to turn the burden of government over to him.

They had reason to be proud of William, son of Robert the Devil, for at fifteen he was tall, with stately bearing, and outstanding among the youths who received the King's honors.

After the ceremony of the accolade there began the exciting, colorful part of the day. Before pavilions decked with banners and glistening shields, there were jousts and tournaments and games of war, as well as a breath-taking display of the accomplishments of both old and new knights of the King's court.

William attracted a great deal of attention. He had a strong, handsome face; his shoulders and arms were powerful, his back was straight and his neck thick-set.

"There is a prince born to be a king," said one wise old Frenchman as he glanced at William in admiration. "He wins every tournament he enters. Who is he?"

"Scarcely a prince," replied his companion drily;

and he took some delight in telling the story of this baseborn knight.

The old Frenchman shook his head wonderingly. Just then William, in full scale armor, sprang on the back of his battle horse without the aid of the stirrup. The huge steed reared and his powerful legs thrashed the air; William struggled to master the animal and in a moment they were thundering across the field.

"I say he was born to be a king," persisted the old warrior.

"More likely for a short life," corrected his companion.

But William, the new Duke of Normandy, was a fighter by nature and he decided, upon his return home, to govern the country himself. He showed his good sense, however, by asking the advice of wise and loyal friends and counselors, Raoul de Vace and William Fitzosbern.

He first commanded his barons to lay down their arms. Couriers bearing his shields and banners went deep into the countryside so that not a village or a town was missed. Every forest hamlet received a warning that severe punishment would be handed out to all those who plundered, murdered, or lived lawlessly.

William's return and his first stern measures only fanned the hatred of some of the disloyal barons. They immediately began to plot against him. But news travels fast and the young Duke had many loyal subjects who lost no time in warning him.

William held a council with his advisors. Before long the roads leading to the ducal court were dotted with little parties of mounted men, many of them in full armor. These were the barons of Normandy, riding out from their castles with their attendants and men-at-arms. Once more they had been summoned by their liege-lord to attend a Great Council in order to make a second oath of allegiance to William, son of Robert the Devil.

This time, in the crowded Great Hall, William wore the robes of state, and when the barons came forward to place their hands between his he towered over them. There was something about his quiet confidence that made them realize that he was ready for a man's responsibilities although still in his teens.

There were many in the gathering who were jealous of his power and who hated him. Among these was a small but powerful group of barons from Western Normandy. One of his own kinsmen, Guy of Burgundy, considered himself the rightful heir to the duchy and had gathered about him a group of supporters.

While words of allegiance rang out in the Great Hall, and the barons placed their hands between those of the young Duke, a plot for the young incumbent's death was already being formed in the minds of the traitorous barons.

Because of this, it was not long before William had a chance to *win* the golden spurs that he was wearing.

CHAPTER V

WINNING THE SPURS
OF KNIGHTHOOD

For some time the barons of western Normandy had been waiting for just the right moment to strike at William. The ungrateful Guy of Burgundy—he had grown up a close friend of William's and had been given more than one lordship with much valuable land—along with the rebels Grimoult, Hamond-with-the-Teeth, Neel and Renulf, were secretly hoarding arms and strengthening their castles.

For weeks their men worked to deepen the moats

and fortify the keeps. The castles rang with the sound of metal work as weapons were repaired and made strong. The kitchens and halls bustled with activity as the Norman ladies planned for food and supervised a hundred and one tasks. Every man-servant was pledged to secrecy. The traveling merchant and weary pilgrim found that at these castles they were not as welcome as usual and were given no more than a place at the hearth for the night, for fear the conspiracy might be revealed.

But William had many friends in this district and the warning of these plots reached him. However, he especially liked to hunt in the forests surrounding his castle at Valognes, and one day he rode there, taking his varlets and squires but foolishly going without an escort of soldiers.

This was the moment for which the traitorous barons had been waiting. Guy of Burgundy received the news that William was nearby and unprotected. Messengers galloped from one end of the district to the other. Hauberks were donned, swords were buckled on and shields slung into place. The speediest horses were quickly saddled.

In one of the stables not far from the castle of Valognes, Gallet the fool was awakened from his sleep. He overheard the plans for William's murder and, being loyal to the Duke, immediately took action. He did not dare to steal a horse from the stable but crept out into the night and ran for all he was worth. No one missed him, and while the mounted parties awaited the arrival of the others, Gallet was able to reach the castle where William was staying.

The breathless Gallet was admitted to the keep and he ran as fast as he could to William's chamber. He shook the Duke and blurted out his story in terror.

William sprang from the bed, dazed and alarmed. Without waiting to put on any more than his shirt and hose and a mantle flung hastily over his shoulders, he grabbed his sword and fled from the castle.

As he leapt on his horse and galloped over the drawbridge, the murderers' horses could be heard thundering toward the castle. Before long they rushed into the keep, swords drawn. The servants were terrified, but Gallet the fool was beside himself with excitement as he shouted at the intruders that they had lost their prey.

The traitors searched the castle thoroughly. This delay gave William a chance to gain ground. His horse seemed scarcely to touch the ground as he galloped on in the bright moonlight. He managed to cross the ford of the river Vire which would soon have held him prisoner by the rising inlet tide.

He reached the village of Ryes by early morning and there was recognized by Hubert, the Lord of Ryes. Hubert took him into his castle, gave him food and clothes and sent him on his way under the escort of his three loyal sons.

When the traitors arrived, Hubert pretended to be in sympathy with them and offered to lead them in the direction that William had taken. He led them at a merciless pace but not the way William had escaped. He played his part so well that the traitorous barons did not know they had been betrayed. Once more young William's life had been saved.

William's loyal and faithful subjects in Falaise were wild with anger when they heard of the traitors' attack upon their lord duke. Life was a very uncertain affair for them; they had to fight in order to eat and survive, and they looked upon William as their protector. The rumor spread all over the city that William had been killed. They knew that the rebels had seized much of his territory and had gone so far as to pronounce him dethroned. The terrifying news of his death made the peasants groan and bewail their great loss.

Then messengers came riding into the city with the truth.

"William lives! He escaped the traitors and is safe!"

The cry went up and soon all of Falaise was overjoyed. When the call went out for help to put the castle of Falaise into a state of defense, every ablebodied person rushed with offers to support William's cause.

Wisely, young William, now forced to take an offensive position against the traitors, hurried off to France to seek Henry's aid. Although his knights and soldiers were the pick of the country they were outnumbered by the traitors.

In pleading for the King's help, William said, "Sire, we have come to seek reward for the loyal service of my father to you, his overlord!"

Robert had helped Henry to defend France against invaders. Now Henry could scarcely reject the pleas of a loyal vassal. Even at the age of twenty, the young Duke was proving himself to be a wise statesman.

Henry, King of France, marched into Normandy with three thousand hand-picked warriors. With all their followers, it is supposed that at least ten thousand set out upon the roads for the Norman duchy. For many miles the sun caught the gleaming breastplates of the warriors and the fluttering banners of the lances in a brilliant display of men and arms. People knelt by the stone crosses which marked the chalky roads, hailing their overlord as the troops moved on, and praying that their lord Duke William would at last win Normandy for himself and for their peace.

In the meantime William had been gathering

his loyal barons about him. They were the best of the Norman stock, hard and ambitious and, like Roger of Sicily, "furious in battle," the type of soldier who would later follow William in his invasion of England. They were trained men and well equipped. The Normans used the hauberk, a close-fitting garment of linen or leather with leggings attached and covered with metal plates in the shape of scales. This covered the wearer from neck to knees. On their heads was a covering called a *camail* which pro- tected most of the face and all of the neck; and over this was worn the conical Norman helmet with its long metal nose protector.

The Norman rode a horse which was handsomely caparisoned, and his weapons were a ten-foot lance with iron head, a great cross-hilted sword, a mace and an axe. His shield was large and pear-shaped. Thus equipped, the Norman knight was a figure of dread and a lethal opponent. A charge of Norman horsemen could be compared only to an avalanche.

When the French King arrived with his army, the Norman forces of the young Duke were camped at the River Muance. The rebels had taken up their position on a wide level plain close at hand and seemed disposed to give battle. Henry and his chief advisors rode out with young William to look over the enemy dispositions. At first there was some shaking of heads, because the enemy seemed strongly placed. It was William who pointed out the vulnerability of their position. The river took a deep bend behind the rebel lines and there was a cover of trees between. They had no line of retreat!

Through the hours of the night William sat as close to the enemy lines as he dared, fearful that they would attempt to get away under cover of darkness. In the morning the mists cleared, and there stood the rebel barons, ready to give battle. After attending Mass, the young Duke moved to the head of his troops. This would be his baptism of fire.

William and Henry were conferring together when they saw, out of the mists, a party of mounted soldiers approaching from the distance. It was a magnificent squadron of more than a hundred knights, with a commander in gleaming hauberk who rode a coal-black battle horse.

"Who are these?" the King demanded to know, as the party moved toward the entrance to Val-des-Dunes. "Have they come to join us, or are they with the enemy?"

Everyone was asking the same question.

"It is Raoul Tasisson, Lord of Cinglais," replied William, his eyes squinting and his face thoughtful.

"By God's truth, I have seldom seen a finer body of men!" said the King with enthusiasm.

There was a silence as the squadron moved on, and a moment of suspense as the troops advanced toward the fork of the road. There they must either wheel in order to join the rebels, or press on toward the loyal troops gathered under the standard of the golden leopards and the cross of Normandy.

"I swear to heaven I have never done Raoul Tasisson wrong. I have been friend to him as well as ruler," said William in a low voice. "But only God knows whether he fights with us or with Guy of Burgundy!"

Now the leader of the squadron had passed the fork in the road and the troops followed, heading for William. The young ruler sat on his war horse like a statue, awaiting the leader, Raoul Tasisson. His face was set and his keen eyes did not move from the approaching commander. The soldiers around him were alerted, their hands on their swords.

Tasisson rode forward, a smile on his face. His right arm was extended as he pulled up beside William, and he struck the young ruler on the shoulder lightly with his clenched fist.

"There, I have struck you, my lord Duke!" he exclaimed, his voice ringing out so that all could hear.

"I swore that I would strike at you, and strike you I did. And now I would strike your enemies, those who beguiled me into their ranks."

He drew out his sword and flourished it in a gesture of fealty, pledging himself to the young Duke. Every knight behind him joined in this act of allegiance. Their voices rang out and finally all ranks, French and Norman, joined in the cry, shouting out their loyalty and calling upon God to defend

the right.

Now the three commanders, Henry, William and
Tasisson, drew up plans of attack. The arrival of
these fighters heightened the excitement and suspense. Raoul had come very close to joining the
rebels. He had been talked into siding with them
but when he saw the banners of Normandy with
their gold leopards, and the gleaming shields of the
loyal soldiers in the distance, he regretted his treach-

ery and longed to fight with the Duke. Calling his troops to a halt, he frankly told them that he could not strike against William, and asked their advice. As a man they shouted, "We fight with William!"

The battles of Val-des-Dunes was a tremendous clash of sword and lance and mace, in hand-to-hand fighting. In the dust of the plain William fought in the center of his men, his great sword crashing down on the helmets of those who attacked. French and Norman and traitor fought on rearing, plunging horses. Over the clash of sword and shield came the cry of the Normans, *"Dieu aide!"* and the French soldier's *"Montjoie!"* while the rebels called upon the saints to help them.

No man fought with more skill or daring than the young Duke. He was fearless in his first taste of real battle, and on this day, with one stroke, he brought down the mightiest warrior of Bayeux, which was really the beginning of the rebels' defeat. Renulf was so terrified that he fled.

The other rebels lost hope when they saw Renulf flying for his life. But the only retreat was toward the River Bully, and it was swollen, with steep muddy banks on each side. The men and horses slid and floundered by the hundred, falling into the river where the current carried them downstream. It is said that the river became so dammed up with bodies that the wheels of the mills stopped turning.

Four of the rebel knights escaped, but they never again regained power in Normandy. This was the end of their revolt. William had won the gilded spurs of knighthood. And all of Normandy was to hear how its young ruler had fought surrounded by his men, a strong and daring warrior. From this day on, men began to fear him and respect him as their ruler.

CHAPTER VI

TROUBLE WITH
THE BARONS

This was by no means the end of the young Duke's troubles with his barons, however. One of his own kinsmen claimed that he was the rightful heir to Normandy.

Count d'Argues was the traitor, and William ordered him to come to his court at Rouen to give an account of himself. The insubordinate baron defied William. He had been secretly hoarding arms and ammunition for a long time. He had transformed

his castle into a fortress that was bristling with weapons and soldiers and was well-stocked with food and water.

"Tell my lord Duke," came the impudent message from the Baron, "that when I come to Rouen, it will be to *take* the city. It belongs to me, as does Normandy!"

William was enraged. Even as a young man his violent, passionate anger made those around him tremble. On hearing the message he leapt to his feet, his face livid, his clenched fists raised above his head. "By Heaven, we shall see to whom Normandy belongs! All those who love me, follow me!"

Once more William gathered an army. But he knew of more than one way to conquer. He had proved himself to be a vigorous, aggressive warrior, and now he was to show that he could be as patient as he was belligerent, and a shrewd and wily campaigner as well.

The Count's castle surmounted a huge rock near Dieppe. It stood outlined against the sky, every wall, tower and turret strong and high.

"Let the young upstart attack!" boasted the Count. "Normandy belongs to the true blood of Rollo, not to a baseborn son!"

But William had no thought of carrying the stronghold by assault. He ordered his men to pitch camp. The soldiers were then dispatched to strategic places so that the castle was completely cut off.

Days and weeks passed by. The castle walls and towers still bristled with armed men, but the arrogant castellan had no way of replenishing his supplies. William was content to wait; it was a battle in which not a drop of blood was being shed among his men.

The Count's men were less fortunate. Before long all the supplies were gone and the garrison was starving.

Finally the young Duke sent a herald with a promise of safety for all those within the fort who were willing to surrender. It did not take long for the castle doors to open and the Count's soldiers to straggle out, thin, lifeless men who had once been robust and confident warriors. Many of the women and children were so sick and wasted that they had to be carried out. The Count, who had fared no better than the others, had no more impudent words with which to challenge the grandson of the tanner of Falaise.

This was another victory for William, and from that time on, in 1047, no prince of the blood tried to win power from the Duke of Normandy.

CHAPTER VII

WILLIAM TAKES
A WIFE

The time had come for William to take a wife. He was twenty-one, and established firmly as Duke of Normandy, with a wide and deserved reputation as a just though stern ruler and a warrior of rare courage.

If the King of England, who was known as Edward the Confessor because he was so devout, had possessed a daughter, it is probable that William would have asked for her hand in marriage. This ambitious youth already had his eyes fixed on that fertile island on the other side of the Sleeve, as the French called the English Channel. Whenever his gaze turned to the north, he would fall into a silent mood and his eyes would take on a withdrawn look and his nostrils would flare. England! He coveted that land of plenty, which was so much more bountiful and green than the sometimes arid and sometimes sour lands along the Seine.

But Edward the Confessor had no children, and it happened that the young Duke was at the court of Henry of France one day when Count Baldwin of Flanders arrived with his daughter Matilda. After the first glance at Matilda, William knew she was the only woman he would ever take as a wife.

It is a custom with those who write of history and romance to speak of all princesses as fair. Sometimes they deserve this praise but generally they are just about the same as the daughters of counts and councilors and knights and goldsmiths, even of cooks and kitchen knaves. But in the case of Matilda there could be no doubt that she deserved everything which had been said about her. She had snow-white skin, soft black hair, and eyes of a dusky enchantment. Moreover she was talented. She could embroider and paint, her voice was like the most tender notes of the zither, and she was lively and gay of manner. Her father, Baldwin de Lisle, was wealthy and powerful, with the blood of King Alfred of England and Charlemagne flowing in his veins. Matilda's dowry would be large and her family connections would be valuable to one as farseeing as young William.

If Matilda had been fancy free when she first saw William, she probably would have reciprocated his feeling. He was a commanding figure in his robe of apricot velvet embroidered with gold thread. He wore a heavy gold chain around his neck with the leopard insignia in precious stones, his black hair was uncurled in the Norman fashion and cut straight across his brow, his eyes were dark and bold. His sword with its jeweled hilt dangled against the straightest thigh in the court of Henry that day.

But Matilda, unfortunately, was not fancy free.

Some time before a young man had arrived from England on some mission to her father. Brithric the Saxon was young for such an errand but he was no hobbledehoy; rather, he was a debonair youth with such fair hair and skin that he had been nicknamed Snow. He had a fine and lively eye in his head and an engaging manner. Matilda had fallen in love with the handsome Saxon and had not cared who knew it. She had done everything in her power to keep him from returning to England, wearing her heart on her sleeve and almost, if not quite, throwing herself at his head.

But Brithric was in love with a flaxen-haired lady at home and had plighted his troth to her. He looked at the fair proportions of the lovely Matilda with some regret perhaps but felt that he could not break his word. His mission completed, he returned to England and married the golden damsel of his choice, leaving Matilda to eat out her heart for him.

Her infatuation for the unresponsive Saxon was still so great that Matilda paid no attention to young William of Normandy whose eyes had so boldly challenged hers. In fact she was not interested in

the least when he made it clear that he desired her
for his wife. Her father, on the other hand, ap-
proved of the match. He would undoubtedly have
arranged it without his daughter's consent but a second obstacle cropped up as soon as they reached
the point of drawing the papers. The Church refused consent to the union.

It has been assumed that the stand of Pope Leo
IX was due to a belief that both parties were descended from Rollo through one William Towhead,
Count of Bonthieu, although other explanations have
been advanced. Whatever the reason, the papal atti-
tude could not be changed, much to the relief per-

haps of the lovely Matilda. For seven years William continued his courting of her, never slackening in his devotion or determination.

And now the favorite legend of William as a young man must be told, although there is a tendency in some quarters to say that the incident never occurred. William, according to the story, became convinced that his lady's reluctance was due to his illegitimate birth. He decided then that enough time had been wasted in pleading letters and in arguing the case with a Pope whose mind was made up. He decided to act.

He was starting out for the chase one day when news reached him that Matilda was in her father's chief city of Bruges which lay just over the border.

"Take the hounds back to the kennel," he said to the men about him. "There will be no hunting today." He looked up into the bright Norman sky and added: "The sun will shine tomorrow and the wild boar will still be there. I have other things to do."

With a small train only, and traveling as much as possible by night to avoid notice, William rode to

Bruges. On his arrival, he learned that Matilda the Desirable was attending Mass. His face, which had been growing darker with every stride of his horse, became more set and determined than his men had ever seen it.

"You will await me here!" he said.

The lolling varlets in the doorways of taverns and the neat, plump maidservants who came by on errands for their mistresses noticed the tall grim figure standing silently at the foot of the cathedral steps.

"Who is it?" they asked among themselves.

"It's the Duke William of Normandy," answered one of them.

"Ach, how stern he looks!" declared one of the maidservants.

"And such a handsome young man! What brings him to Bruges and why does he stand there like the stone statue of a saint?"

"The Lady Matilda is within," contributed one of the others.

And so everyone found excuses for delay. People waited about and whispered among themselves and kept their eyes on the ominous figure of the young Duke. An air of expectancy settled over the square in front of the cathedral. Even the breeze died down and there was not as much as the rustle of a leaf on the cobbled streets. The pigeons on the cathedral leads stopped cooing, the town dogs for once did not snap or snarl over bones. Doors neither opened nor closed and faces which appeared at windows remained fixed in the picture.

At last the cathedral door opened and people began to stream down the steps. One of the last to appear was the lovely daughter of the noble Count Baldwin. From under the black wimple which covered her head her eyes detected the unmoving figure at the foot of the steps. She recognized the Duke and her heart gave a flutter. What was his purpose?

William confronted her as her feet touched the flagged stone of the square. The history books do not record what he said to her but it is not hard to imagine the words which rose to his lips.

"Seven years is a long time, my Lady Matilda. For seven years I have held you in my heart, for seven years I have desired you for my wife. It is a

long enough time, my lady, to end the patience of even one who loves as devotedly as I do."

He reached out abruptly and laid his hands on the bright cloak which covered her shoulders. He tore it off, ripped it in two, and threw the remnants on the ground. Then he took her by the shoulders and shook with a passion which had something of devotion in it; his face was hard, his eyes distended. Matilda, frightened for perhaps the first time in her life, fell at his feet. She did not entreat him to spare her, in fact she did not utter a single word.

"I shall wait on your caprices no longer," said William, finally. Turning away, he sprang into the saddle and rode off to join his men.

Perhaps it is from this instance, and many similar ones which can be found in the pages of history, that a belief has come down even to modern times about the best method to be used in courtship. Certainly it has been widely believed that women like to be won by force. Matilda proceeded to add substance to the belief. She made up her mind at once that she wanted to marry William of Normandy after all.

Disregarding the opposition of the Church, they were married in 1053, when William was twenty-six years old and one of the most handsome and virile of bridegrooms to stand before an altar and swear the solemn oaths.

Archbishop Malger of Rouen, the head of the Church in Normandy, made good his threats by excommunicating William. If his subjects had obeyed the rules laid down in cases where the ban of the Church has been applied, William and his bride would have been in a sorry plight. They would have had no servants to wait on them, to prepare their meals, and no armored horsemen to accompany them when they rode out. No one would have spoken to them and they would have been shunned like lepers, as if the very air were polluted by their presence. But an oath of worldly allegiance took precedence over the wrath of the Church, and so life at the Norman court went on much the same as usual.

Two years later there was a new Pope, Nicholas II, and a dispensation for the marriage was granted. William showed his gratitude by building the Abbey of St. Stephen at Caen.

The young Duke and his no longer reluctant bride were very happy. They lived as man and wife in complete content and had many children, including three sons, Robert, William and Henry, of whom more will be told later.

CHAPTER VIII

EDWARD THE CONFESSOR

There had been in England a king named Ethelred who was such a weak and slack ruler that people called him Ethelred the Unready. He was never equal to any task. When the Danes came swarming across the North Sea in their long-prowed ships, the English Navy would be scattered or rusting in harbors and there would be no army ready to face the marauders when they landed. The Danes did as they pleased, harrying the coastal districts, burning and slaying as they went and carrying the young people off as slaves, particularly the flaxen-haired and rosy-cheeked girls. Gradually they overran parts of England and settled down. Ethelred the Unready, unable to meet them and fight it out as a king should, hit upon the idea of buying the invaders off. The first time he paid them ten thousand pounds. Back they came many times, always demanding more Danegeld, as the English called this tax laid upon them. Finally the poor bumbling King had to pay nearly fifty thousand pounds to persuade the Danes to go away.

This was an enormous sum in those days, when a pound was worth at least a hundred modern dollars, and to raise it the people of England had to be taxed almost to the last penny they possessed. Finally they began to feel they would rather let the Danes stay than pay the exactions put on them by their absurd misfit of a king. When the final invasion came about under a Danish king named Sweyn, they were relieved that their king (who had even been known to be late for the hunt and who was invariably late for a great banquet) had at last been prompt in answering one Summons. Ethelred the Unready had died. What reward would heaven have for an unready king? The people did not care.

Sweyn's son Canute became King of England. He was strong and intelligent as well as a brave man. He married Emma, the beautiful Norman widow of Ethelred, and she became completely devoted to him. She had brought two sons into the world while married to Ethelred and the older of the pair, Edward, had lost no time in crossing the Channel to Normandy when the Danish wave engulfed the country. He grew up there and became a thorough Norman in habit and outlook. Nevertheless when Canute and his sons died, the English Witenagemot (the forerunner of the modern parliament) invited Edward to come back and take the throne. He accepted the summons and brought a whole train of Normans into England with him.

A curious individual, this Edward who became known as the Confessor in history. He was frail of physique, with white hair and a long white beard and hands so long and thin that they seemed almost transparent. He was full of contradictions, spending hours each day at his devotions and then rushing off to the hunt with a furious appetite to kill the poor wild creatures of the forest. He was gentle to those about him but ready to order fire and sword for any part of his kingdom which showed an independent spirit. He would have been as weak a king as his unready sire if there had not been in England at that time one of those strong men who win for themselves the title of kingmaker.

Earl Godwine of the West Saxons took matters in hand and arranged for Edward to marry his handsome daughter Edytha while he and his strong sons, particularly Harold the first-born, ruled the country. Edward neglected Edytha and produced no sons and he seemed content to spend most of his time in the oratory. He stood out, however, in demanding the best of everything for the Normans he had brought back with him. He made them councilors and stallers (a Saxon term for a court official) and he filled the high offices of the church with them, making three of them bishops and finally choosing one as Archbishop of Canterbury. When Godwine stood out against these appointments, the

frail King ordered him into exile with all of his family. But Godwine came back with a strong army behind him and the second unready King gave in, accepting Godwine back and cheerfully enough allowing him to resume the reins of office.

William of Normandy, shrewd and far-seeing William, had been keeping an eye on the way things were going in England. At this point, two years before he persuaded Matilda to marry him, he decided to pay a visit to this kinsman who was showing such a preference for everything Norman. He took a fleet of ships with him, with Norman banners fluttering from the mastheads and gleaming shields slung over the sides which bore the ducal arms. The reception he received was warm and flattering. Edward was delighted with this young kinsman who was so strong and determined and who had already won so great a reputation.

There could be no sharper contrast than the two rulers offered even though they were openly on the very best of terms. The frail, thin-shanked Edward went hunting with the tall and powerfully thewed, William and was amazed at his cousin's skill. He fingered the bow which no one could draw save William and he sat in long discussions with the Duke, amazed at his decision and clarity of mind.

The Norman followers of the Duke were noticing other contrasts. They looked at the green fields and the rich crops, they counted the fat cattle in the meadows and the woolly sheep on the hillsides, and they marveled at such plenty. "Why," they asked themselves, "did Rollo pass by the Thames and elect to make his landing instead at the mouth of the Seine?" Perhaps, they thought, their sturdy young Duke would see a way to correct Rollo's mistake.

William's mind, needless to state, was filled with the same dream. To be a king, and of such a rich land as England! Here was Edward, sickly and falling rapidly into a decline, with no direct heirs of his own save a cousin of some degree who had fled to Hungary for sanctuary. Why should not he, William, succeed to the throne when the thin hands of the Confessor were folded over his chest for the last, long sleep? Certainly the devout King was showing him every preference. William sat beside him on a dais and under a canopy of gold cloth. He was being fed four times a day on the finest delicacies England could provide. None but Normans shared the royal table and none others fed off gold dishes and drank from cups inlaid with jewels; not even the watchful Godwine and his resolute sons. Edward made it clear that he was happy when he sat thus in the company of these strangers.

But William always kept his feet on the ground and the thoughts which filled his mind were realistic. He knew that the succession to the English throne was decided in the Witenagemot, where the influence of Godwine was supreme. These English churls, he said to himself, were above themselves, thinking it their right to deny a son the throne of his father if they saw fit; or a foreign kinsman when there was no son to claim the succession. In Normandy it was different. In the land of the pirates men had no such rights. In fact common men had no rights at all, save to labor for their overlord and die for their duke. Rollo had established an absolute form of rule. But all William could hope to have in England was the promise of Edward. With that as his justification, he could come back and conquer

England, if Englishmen refused to recognize his right. They would have no rule thereafter save the iron law of their Norman master. The Witenagemot would become a dim memory of the past.

No one knows just what did take place on that visit to England between Edward and William, but later William swore that a promise had been given him. In his writings he spoke of having paid homage to Edward. Evidently he went back to Normandy quite satisfied that he had a claim to the English crown.

The golden, dragon-prowed ships set their course for home with a young man of twenty-four watching the cliffs of Dover grow fainter and fainter as he stood at the stern of the leading vessel. The horizon blotted out the shoreline, and with the Norman love of oaths, he murmured to himself, "By God's splendor, the Norman ceorl who follows me there shall become an earl on English soil. Saxons will share their wealth of land and gold with the Norman, and our conquering race will make an empire there. And William will be king!"

CHAPTER IX

WILLIAM TRAPS A RIVAL

To succeed in plans as daring as those which filled the mind of William of Normandy, a man had to take chances, and therefore had to be lucky. Everything was breaking in Napoleon's favor, for instance, when he was at the peak of his conquering career. The rains came when he needed them and held off when dry roads were essential. His opponents made all the mistakes he expected them to make. But with the retreat from Moscow the reverse became true and ill luck dogged him to his final defeat.

At first William thought the breaks of the game were all going against him because Edward the Confessor continued to live on and on, long after his end had been predicted. Whenever a Norman returned from London William would take him aside and ask, "How goes it with my cousin in England?" and the reply would invariably be the same. Edward would die any day, at any hour even. But the frail old man continued to live nevertheless; and the temper of the Duke grew short when his mind dwelt on this matter. Then, thirteen years after his visit to Edward's court, something happened, something most unexpected. When William heard of it, he knew that the Goddess of Luck had finally decided to favor him.

A Saxon ship had been wrecked off the Norman coast and only a handful of those on board had been rescued. One of the survivors was the owner of the vessel, a handsome and golden-haired man of middle years who acknowledged that he was Harold Godwineson! The man who was known to be William's chief rival for the English throne was in his power! Harold, it developed, had fallen into the hands of Count Guy of Ponthieu, a designing nobleman who had promptly locked the English earl and his younger brother Wulnoth, as well as several English knights, into prison cells in his castle. They were being held for high ransom. Guy of Ponthieu was a Norman of Normans and he knew that Harold would claim the crown as soon as the old wraith of a king died. Before he could feather his nest by collecting the ransom money, however, William descended upon him with an armed force at his back and righteous fire in his eye. By what right, he demanded, did the Count of Ponthieu hold Harold of the West Saxons in a malefactor's cell? What infamous conduct was this?

Reluctantly Guy of Ponthieu parted with his prisoners, knowing full well that William himself intended to reap a golden harvest from this favorable chance. The Duke saw to it that Harold and all his men were treated royally. They were released from their vile and cramped cells, were bathed and anointed and dressed in rich raiment, and taken to

Rouen where they were feasted like kings. On the surface there was nothing but good will between them.

But Harold knew from the first instant that he had fallen into a trap. Much better for him the rat-infested cell at Ponthieu, with his release certain, than to bask in William's company! Being a schemer himself, he could understand the wily plan in William's mind. Intensely ambitious also, he could understand that the Norman Duke would go to any lengths to squeeze every advantage out of this situation. Outwardly, of course, the two men were most cordial to each other. They hunted together and hawked together, and sat side by side at the Duke's table.

Harold kept protesting that he had been away from England overlong, that his administrative duties demanded his immediate return. William smiled and nodded—and organized more hunts and tournaments for Harold's entertainment. When he led an invading army into Brittany Harold went with him. The English Earl fought bravely in the front rank of the attack, matching William in the valor of his efforts. Weeks went by. Months passed.

And still Harold remained the unwilling guest of the Norman Duke.

The Duke of the Normans could not help but admire and respect this Saxon with his majestic bearing and gallantry. He even made Harold a knight, heaping him with the highest Norman honors. It was agreed that someday he would become his kinsman with the promise of one of William's daughters in marriage.

William, of course, regarded himself as the legal successor to Edward. He was a cautious far-seeing man and he knew well that Harold was powerful in England, revered by the people and looked upon as a great leader. He must be sure that Harold would not be an obstacle in his future plans.

The issue between them probably had never been expressed but both men understood it. Harold could return to England when he agreed to support William as successor to Edward's throne; and not before. This was openly understood, in England as well as in Normandy.

Finally Harold, having no alternative, gave in. He agreed to William's terms.

The Duke staged an elaborate ceremony. The whole world, by which he meant western Europe, must know what happened. The Great Hall was filled with witnesses when the Anglo-Saxon Earl entered. He was conducted to a chest covered with cloth of gold, upon which rested a missal. The words of the oath he must swear had been prepared for him and Harold uttered them in a loud tone which could be heard by all present. The Norman barons repeated after him in sonorous tones, "May God be my Help."

And then William played his trump card. He strode to the chest, removed the missal and whisked off the cloth-of-gold covering. The chest underneath was filled with the relics of saints. Bones white with age, fearsome in their significance, they testified to the solemnity of the oath to which the Englishman had sworn.

Harold turned pale. He realized how completely William had trapped him. An oath was a sacred matter to men of that age, not only a promise made between men but a covenant with God. The Church looked with the utmost severity on any breach of an oath, and sometimes the punishment was excommunication.

Harold could feel scores of cold Norman eyes on him as he stood there and looked down into the satin-covered nest where the dry bones lay. There was a calculating gleam in all of those eyes, an exultant gleam. Perhaps a vision came to him of the certain result of this oath he had sworn over the time-hallowed bones of the saints. Perhaps he heard

faintly the battle cry of Normandy as the armed knights of William charged up the slopes of Hastings. He may even have felt the terror of arrows raining from the sky, one of which carried death for him on its iron point!

CHAPTER X

HAROLD OF WESSEX
BECOMES A KING

Edward the Confessor lay dying. His long white
hands were folded upon his bosom and the gray
pallor of death had touched his features. Edytha,
his wife, stood close beside the massive bed; the
room beyond was crowded with the King's ecclesi-
astics and men of state.

There was a hush in the room, for Edward was
speaking in a whispered, labored voice. Those around
the deathbed strained to hear what he was saying.

† 85 †

Edward, in the visions and dreams of his last days, had been predicting dire things for England. Fire and the sword were to fall upon the whole land. The blood of loyal Englishmen was to gush forth like a river, and all the people were to be bowed down with the yoke of oppression.

Not only were the clergy and noblemen clustered around the King's bed eager to hear every last word of prophecy, but the people crowding the court-yards of Westminster Palace as well. Their concern was not so much for the loss of their King as for their future. Who would be England's next King? Who would lead them in the time of this threatened bloodshed and crushing oppression?

As they stood in a drizzling rain, waiting for the bells to toll, for the words *The King is dead!* to be passed through the crowds, Edward was speaking of England and its throne. His weak, faltering voice seemed to take on strength as he spoke to the nobleman who knelt by his bed.

"I commend my wife into your hands. Serve her and protect her. And into your hands I commend my kingdom. Lead my people and defend them."

The nobleman kneeling at his bedside was Harold, Earl of Wessex, the man who had pledged to support the Duke of Normandy. Harold was the man whom loyal Saxons had long been clamoring for—Harold, who had been so close to the King during his last years.

Now as Edward's frail hand was upon him in a blessing, Harold was no longer William's *man.* The oath to the Norman Duke belonged to the past. Edward in his last hours had either changed his mind about William as his successor, or was proving that he had never given the promise claimed by the Duke. Harold, the loyal Saxon, was his choice.

The Great Council wanted Harold, too. The day after Edward's death, in January, 1066, Harold was crowned in Westminster Abbey, the church that Edward had built and his only great personal achievement of a lifetime. All of England rejoiced. There was not a drop of royal blood in Harold's veins but the English needed a strong leader, and Harold had governed for the King with a tolerance and forebearance unusual in those days of cruelty. He was wise and firm, and he was a magnificent warrior, the only man who could defend England.

So Harold was anointed with holy oil and the crown of England was placed upon his head. His country needed him, therefore his oath to William was wiped out. He felt free to accept the decision of the Council, for his oath had been made under force. He, not the baseborn son of Robert the Devil, was to be King of England.

However, Harold knew that the Norman ruler

would strike back. He began to prepare for the attack the day after he was crowned.

William was at his hunting seat of Quivilly the morning the news came from England. It was a crisp winter's day and the hounds were yelping in anticipation of the hunt. Varlets and grooms scurried around preparing the horses and checking on the hunting bows and arrows. William had arrived by boat from his castle across the Seine and was standing with his massive bow on his shoulder when a breathless messenger came hurrying up from the river. He went straight to the Duke and gave him a message in a low voice. "Edward, King of England, is dead. Harold of Wessex has been crowned as his successor!"

William stood for a moment, as if stunned. He questioned the messenger briefly, and then his voice rang out, cursing Harold, defaming the Saxon knight with such terrible oaths that the noblemen and attendants blanched at his words and at the sight of their enraged Duke. Then, his face livid, William strode to the river and set out for the castle, without a word or a glance at anyone.

In the castle, he shut himself away and would not speak. Not one of the household dared approach him. He paced up and down the stone floor of his chamber like a caged lion. Finally, his close friend and seneschal (the chief steward of his ducal household) dared to enter the chamber. He boldly urged the Duke to cease his brooding and to act instead, attack the Saxon and punish him for his disloyalty, his treachery!

This advice seemed to break the spell of William's rage and the Duke sprang into action. A messenger was sent on a journey to London, with all possible speed, bearing a command from the Norman Duke that Harold should at once fulfil his oath to William.

There were many long days of suspense before word came back from England. Relays of messengers had to ride day and night, a channel vessel had to wait until tide and wind were favorable, before Normandy learned Harold's answer. Meanwhile the ducal court buzzed with all kinds of rumors. Talk of war was spreading to all corners of the kingdom.

Harold's reply was one of defiance. He was no longer William's man but the rightful King of England, the choice of the people! Immediately William called an assembly of the Norman barons to meet at Lillebonne. He would invade England, punish the traitor, and take the throne and the crown that Harold had seized. This announcement of policy was received with enthusiastic approval. The barons of Normandy wanted nothing better than a chance to seize the rich lands of England.

CHAPTER XI

THE NORMANS MAKE PLANS TO INVADE ENGLAND

The sentiment in Normandy was favorable to the bold course but it quickly developed that William's barons, being Norman and therefore pretty careful about spending their money, did not respond to the need of paying the costs of such a huge venture. The leaders among them even held a secret meeting to discuss the matter. They made sure that William Fitzosbern, called William of the Bold Heart, was present to hear what they had to say.

This William Fitzosbern, who was destined to play a great part in the events which followed and to be remembered in English history, was Duke William's closest friend and adviser. He was, moreover, the chief officer of the royal household. It seemed certain that, if the Normans invaded England, William of the Bold Heart would be the Duke's right-hand man, serving perhaps in the capacity known as chief of staff in a modern army. It had been Fitzosbern who had gone to the Duke first to urge that he gird on his armor and punish Harold for his perfidy.

The upshot of this meeting was that the canny barons delegated Fitzosbern to go to the Duke and tell him that they would not meet the exactions he was laying on their shoulders. They could not raise the armed forces they were expected to bring into the field nor pay for ships which the Duke had allotted to them. They were prepared to fight but he must pay the cost of the invasion himself.

Now Fitzosbern was fully as determined as William and he took to his liege lord a much different report of the temper of the barons. He told the Duke that they were not only willing to do everything asked of them but that they would double the number of armed men they had been asked for and the ships they were supposed to contribute.

The Duke, needless to state, was delighted with this report and plunged at once into the labor of organizing his invasion forces. When whispers began to reach his ears that his lieutenant's report had been optimistic, to say the least, William met the situation with promises. He would divide all the fine green lands of England and the teeming streams among those who fought with him and had contributed to the cost. The larger the contribution, the more free land. The selfish instincts of the Normans were roused to a high peak by these promises. Their reluctance was broken down.

William took another step which served his purposes well. He sent a message to the Pope and secured the support of the pontiff for his venture, basing his claim on the promise made by Edward the Confessor and on the oath of Harold. Some of the cardinals were against taking a stand but the

Pope, Alexander II, made the decision in favor of the Norman claims. He sent his blessing to William, together with a ring, a relic of St. Peter, and a consecrated banner. This made it possible for Duke William to proclaim the invasion of England a Holy Crusade. Emboldened by the papal support, the Normans enlisted freely and volunteers from other lands began to flock into Normandy to enlist under the leopard flag. There were always trained mercenaries in Europe, professional soldiers who sold their services to the highest bidder. These cruel birds of prey came flocking to the Norman flag, eager to have a hand in the despoiling of the island kingdom.

The die had been cast. Immediately the seaports of Normandy became hives of industry. The number of ships assembled for the invasion has been variously estimated. Some historians say William had 700 ships, some say 3,000. Ordinarily the larger estimate could safely enough be declared an exaggeration but in this case it was probably not far from the truth. William was planning to take over a large army. Some authorities say he had 25,000 fighting men, knights and foot soldiers and archers, some put the total even higher. This, of course, was only the fighting half. In addition there would be servants and cooks and mechanics and mule drivers, and camp followers of all descriptions; almost as many again.

The ships of that day were quite small and a great number would be needed to transport an army of this size, particularly as they would have to take over thousands of horses and great supplies of arms and such necessary equipment as transport wagons, tents, forges, and a large supply of food as well. To live off the land an army must be on the move and must be free to forage over a wide area. William could not be sure that he would find it possible to spread his forces thin enough for that, with the English army ready to pounce upon them; and so he had to take large supplies of food as well as everything else.

And so the little ports rang with the sounds of a feverish activity. Sparks rose from the forges and the screech of saws filled the air. Forests were leveled to get tree trunks for the masts, and trains of patient mules were used to drag the great logs to the shops where they would be trimmed and sized. The sound of the Norman axes could not be heard across the Channel but the English had spies in Normandy and word reached them early of the blow William was preparing. Harold organized his army and his fleet, and waited for the fateful day when the blow would fall.

Only a small part of the invasion fleet was made up of the great dragon ships of the Vikings, the war galleys which sometimes had thirty rowing benches and so must have been close to two hundred feet long. The dragons were a beautiful sight when elaborately fitted out with large square sails of bright colors, with the serpent of the North embroidered on them in velvet, with gold on the beaks and the dragon tails. William could not afford such ostentation as that. His sails were of plain cloth with only the leopards of Normandy boldly marked on them. The galleys were stoutly made, however, with the finest of oaken planks, and the heaviest canvas that could be raised at night like a tent (the mast being lowered to serve as ridgepole) and the sides knotted to the gunwales. Every practical detail was attended to with the closest fidelity. The transverse tillers for the steersmen had been hewed from the stoutest giants of the forest and at night the oar ports were closed tightly with circular shutters to keep the sea from breaking in.

William needed dragon ships because he expected that the English fleet would give battle as soon as the invaders endeavored to cross the Channel. Most of the ships he built, however, were of the third class, small sailing vessels called knauships or knorrs. These were for the transport of the horses and the supplies; and they would be loaded to the gunwales and so would be low in the water and clumsy to maneuver. William's plan undoubtedly was to keep these small vessels in the center and the dragon fleet on the flanks to beat off the English if they came out.

With such a taskmaster to urge them on, and the watchful William Fitzosbern of the Bold Heart to keep an eye on them, the shipbuilders and the carpenters and the blacksmiths never relaxed in their efforts. And quickly a great fleet was assembled in

the estuary of the Dive which William had chosen as the port of embarkation.

When the news reached England, the people flocked to the churches and prayed loudly to the Lord who sat far above earthly kings, begging His compassion and His help. Harold, beset by difficulties and jealousies, had to keep watch along the whole southern coast of England, not knowing where the blow would fall. And he had to keep his war vessels cruising in the North Sea against the threat of another invasion from Norway. The outlook was black indeed for the defenders.

But William took a long time in starting. In those days there were no instruments to guide ships at sea and the steersmen had to depend on the sun and stars for their direction, particularly the pole star at nights. Sometimes they resorted to such crude devices as measuring the shadow cast by the gunwales on the rowing seats. When the sky was overcast, they were pretty much at a loss and had to depend on loosing flocks of sea-going birds. The course the birds took would then be followed because they would strike for the nearest land.

But even when the sun was out the sailors of that day worked under great difficulties. They knew little of navigation. The Viking ships were fast when the wind was abeam but the rigidity of the one sail made it necessary to have a favorable breeze if they expected to make any headway.

So William and his army and his great fleet of little ships filling the mouth of the Dive had to wait with such patience as they could summon up for the winds which would carry them across the Channel. The favorable winds were a long time in coming.

The Duke had to practice patience. For fifteen days the weather kept the Norman leader in its power. Each morning William arose from his bed with the dawn to look out at the weather vane. It swung merrily in the breeze while the Duke chafed at the delay. All eyes were focused on its movement with each new gust of wind. Masses were sung daily; but still the tyrannical winds kept this mighty army at bay.

Finally with the dawn of September 27th, 1066, the weather vane swung around. The first words that greeted the Duke were, "The wind has taken a turn, sire Duke!" Excitement swept through the port. Now the time had come for the move so carefully planned by the Duke in his game of winning an empire.

The first ship that set sail for England was the *Mora,* William's flagship, a beautiful golden vessel which was a present from his wife. The stately *Mora* flew the Pope's banner as well as the standard

of Normandy, three golden lions upon a white background. As the billowing sail carried her out to sea, the bow of the ship rose and fell with a figurehead of a boy blowing an ivory trumpet. A lantern swung from the mast, and this was to be the beacon light that directed the ships following in the *Mora's* wake toward the shore of England.

The ships that launched out into the stiff breeze
for which the Normans had been devoutly praying
were loaded with men and horses and equipment.
The *Mora* soon outsailed them, and when the dawn
came it was discovered that she was anchored alone
and unescorted within range of the English shore.
Here was a priceless prize of war, the flagship with

William and his staff officers aboard. But the Royal Navy was not there to swoop down upon her out of the morning mist. King Harold had ordered his ships to port and dispersed his crews so that they could go back to the land where they were needed for the harvests.

Before long the danger was over. Norman transport ships by the dozens soon caught up with the *Mora* and they sailed on together, descending on the beaches of Pevensey. There was no resistance when these dragon ships from the "land of the pirates" touched England's shores. Thousands of archers with their cropped heads and smocks swarmed out of the ships on that day of September 28th. The beaches were black with horses and baggage, thousands of lances with fluttering ribbons, firebrands, bows and arrows, the very finest fighting equipment that an eleventh-century army could muster.

William had ordered his carpenters to bring along three fortresses of wood, ready to be set up in England. These were quickly erected. A huge moat was dug. Another hasty garrison was made away from the shore, some ten miles from Hastings. Horsemen were ordered off into the countryside to gather up quantities of food for a feast. William, surrounded by many of his chosen knights, set out to reconnoiter. There were no paths, no roads to follow; it was like a wilderness, for all the people had fled for their lives. To the Normans it seemed as if they had taken possession of England already.

Meanwhile Harold and his squadrons of ill-equipped men were racing south to defend their country.

CHAPTER XII

HAROLD'S BATTLE WITH THE VIKINGS

Harold of England had other difficulties to face besides the Norman invasion. Some years before the death of Edward the Confessor he had agreed to the deposing of his brother Tostig as Earl of Northumberland. Tostig seems to have been a thoroughly unworthy son of the great Earl Godwine, and the people had clamored to be free of his rule. After being sent into exile, Tostig seems to have concentrated his hatred on his strong and worthy brother

Harold. His spleen was so deep-seated that he had even gone to Normandy to urge that Duke William assert by arms his nebulous claim to the English throne; a step completely unnecessary, as has already been demonstrated. Tostig then decided on more direct action and he managed to persuade the King of Norway, the great Harold Hardrada, to gather an army and seize the English throne for himself.

Harold Hardrada is one of the great figures in the legends of the Viking kings. He was a blond giant

of enormous strength who was happy only when he was fighting. He was the kind of warrior who sang wild and passionate songs as he went into battle, and it was believed that no other man could wield the battle-axe he used. Tostig's treacherous tongue convinced this picturesque madman that England was ripe for the plucking. Very soon after Harold of Wessex had been crowned king, the Norse menace landed with a large army at the Humber River in the north of England.

This, of course, was before the Norman army of invasion had landed and so King Harold marched north to give battle to the Norsemen. It was because of this diversion in the north that William of Normandy was able to land at Pevensey without any opposition. The result of the Norman invasion might have been different if the Anglo-Saxons had been able to oppose William with the whole English fleet and army.

The two Harolds met at Stamfordbridge. Before beginning the attack the sagacious English King made an effort to avoid bloodshed. He sent a herald out between the lines to propose a negotiated peace to his brother Tostig.

"Where is Tostig, son of Godwine?" demanded the herald.

When the traitor stepped forward and identified himself, the herald offered him in Harold's name peace, friendship and his former lands and possessions.

"What does he offer my ally, the noble King Harold who is called Harold Hardrada?" asked Tostig.

"Seven feet of good English earth," was the answer.

Tostig refused to desert the Viking leader and so the battle was fought. Harold Hardrada was a brave warrior but not a very wise general. He had not disposed his forces to the best advantage and the English won a bloody but decisive victory. The body of the Viking, with an arrow in his throat, was buried in the seven feet of English soil promised him, and the traitor Tostig, who was a shorter man, was laid in less than six feet. It was a costly victory, however, and Harold knew that it had left him much weakened to meet the more serious threat in the south.

The English King was presiding at a victory banquet in the strongly walled city of York when word reached him that William had landed at Pevensey. Leaving his wine cup unemptied, the harassed King rose from the board. In a matter of hours he was marching what was left of his army down the Great North Road.

Englishmen knew little of cavalry fighting at this time, nor did they rely upon their archers. The stalwart Thingmen, the trained troops of King Harold's bodyguard, who fought under the Standard of the Fighting Man, his personal flag, depended mostly upon the battle-axe. William's army, some twenty-five to thirty thousand men, were well-disciplined, battle-hardened fighters. The men marching south with Harold included his army of household guards and as many ploughmen, tradesmen and English youths as the counties could muster. The odds against this exhausted, depleted army were great.

But Harold rode before them, a magnificent figure on his battle horse, despite his exhaustion, the sun gleaming on his fair hair and shining armor; his presence gave them strength for a long forced march southward and courage to face the swarming enemy on their beaches.

CHAPTER XIII

THE NORMANS AND SAXONS PREPARE FOR BATTLE

The Norman army was encamped on a narrow strip of coastal land with the South Downs some six miles to the north. Behind the Downs was the Weald, a grim combination of hills and forests and marshes, with a few small streams pouring down to the Channel. The Weald was almost impassable from a military standpoint. It closed William off from London, unless he elected to make a time-consuming detour along the line of the water into eastern Kent and to strike north from there.

Duke William adopted instead a waiting policy. Occupying London meant nothing unless he had already met and beaten Harold. He might as well remain where he was, forcing Harold to march south and offer battle.

But he could not wait too long. His food supplies were running short. His men were feeling the uncertainty and suspense. The crafty Duke sent them out to lay the countryside bare with fire and sword, hoping that this ruthlessness would force Harold's hand. In the meantime his spies brought him word of the victory Harold had won in the North. Soon afterward news reached him that the English King was marching south in such haste that the sandals of his men were being worn to shreds and even the royal mantle was caked with dust. The Duke knew that Harold would have to pause in London to reorganize his army and secure reinforcements. He prayed earnestly that the Usurper (as he had publicly branded Harold) would come on with little delay.

Each day's delay was serious for the Norman army. The plundered land, a wilderness now, would not even provide a brace of wild fowl, not a pig or a lamb, let alone food for thousands of soldiers. If William pressed on into the country, away from his ships, his position would be threatened. If he withdrew, the rich plum of England that was almost within his grasp would be snatched away.

Suspense was beginning to tell in the countenances of the Norman leaders. Bishop Odo had spoken frankly at council, sharing the thoughts of those who doubted William's ruthless order to ravage the countryside around them. William alone remained confident, a towering figure in a sable cape with jeweled clasps. There was sharpness in his voice, however, when he reassured them.

"I know the man Harold," he told them sternly. "This King of the people is not one to stand by and see Sussex men die and the England of the Saxon lighted by Norman firebrands. God help, he will come. I promise you!"

William Malet, gazing upon the Norman leader,

straightened his shoulders and drew in a full breath of clear, chilled air. He too knew Harold of England. "You speak the truth, my lord Duke. You have drawn him on as a moth to a flame. And he will find the Norman fire hotter than anything of *this* world!"

The grave face of the leader softened into a smile as he nodded, and the men about him relaxed. "Use this night for sleep; for by God's splendor there will be little sleep for Normans when Harold the Usurper comes!"

The group of warriors broke up and soon nothing was to be heard but the occasional bark of a dog and the stirring of the horses in the long lines between the tents.

William's army was in complete readiness for the battle. The foot-soldiers were well armed with shields and swords and maces. The mounted soldiers in their gleaming armor were highly trained, ready with mighty swords and spears. William's archers were supplied with the finest bows and arrows to pierce the hearts of the Saxons who knew little of fighting in any way except in a hand-to-hand battle. The storehouses of the encampment were full to overflowing with firebrands and every instrument of war known to the Normans.

The Norman outpost was at a rise of ground seven miles from the encampment at Hastings, at a place called Telham. This height gave William a position where he could look across to his ships where the Royal Navy might well attack and, beyond a muddy slope and valley, to a spur of land that jutted out from the Downs in a clutter of hills and deep ravines. Spies were posted along the roads leading toward Hastings. At the first sign of fluttering banners or a rise of dust from marching feet and horses, they were to ride with all possible speed to the Duke himself.

Before long it was proved that William did indeed know the English King. A breathless messenger arrived in the camp with the news that a host of men was approaching rapidly.

In the crisp autumn morning the roads were black with riders and marching men. They were headed toward the Downs, under the banner of the Fighting Man. Harold's Thingmen came on foot, bearing battle-axes and kite-shaped shields; his knights in gilded mail armor glistened in the sun; hundreds of rustics followed, laden with every conceivable weapon from spear to wooden club. It was both a noble and a cloddish army coming on steadily after Harold. Their faces were set and gray with battle-fatigue and the strain of the long forced marches. They followed Harold doggedly, ready to spill their blood to drive out the Normans and keep England free.

Wild rumors began to circulate in William's camp as the enemy drew near. Harold was coming with countless numbers. The seas were black with hundreds of vessels bearing down upon the golden dragon ships in the bay. Great engines of war were being dragged toward the Downs which would crush horses and men with their catapulted missiles. More troops were following to the scene with the hard-fighting earls of the North.

At the messenger's first cry of "To arms! The

English are coming!" William had leapt into action, ordering that all foraging parties be called back to camp. He shouted instructions that an advance squadron of fighters must rush to secure the heights of Telham before the English took them.

Harold halted his troops in the lower reaches of the South Downs, some six miles above Hastings. From this high position, he could watch every move made by the invaders. If William divided his army in an effort to move off to the east, he could bide

his time and then strike at their thinning lines. If William chose to fight here, he must fight on Harold's terms; at least he must give battle on ground chosen by the English King for its defensive strength.

Thrice William sent heralds to Harold proposing terms. The only answer he received was a scornful refusal. There was nothing left for William to do but to fight.

William could look across the night and see the English camp outlined against the moonlight. Spear-tips and shields sent forth little darts of light as the men moved about the height opposite. Blurs of white were the tents and pavilions set against the trees beyond.

"By our Lady, we cannot strike while Harold sits like an eagle upon the nest!" the Norman leader exclaimed impatiently.

"He will have taken up a position upon the ridge by morning," his barons pointed out, gravely. "It is folly for us to remain separated from our main force. Let us withdraw quickly."

William, determined to give Harold a chance to come to terms, sent another messenger to Harold's camp. This was Maigrot, a Norman monk, who bore generous offers from the Duke; and when Harold refused, he cried out, challenging him in William's name.

Before all the earls and men present he shouted, "A ban be upon all who fight with Harold! Excommunication and fire everlasting!" These terrible words sent a wave of fear through the ranks of the English, yet Harold did not waver.

When the monk returned with Harold's answer, William knew that the English army would take its stand to the death upon the ridge opposite, while Normans struck over marsh land, ravines and streams to reach them. He gave orders that the whole force be called up from Hastings.

CHAPTER XIV

THE BATTLE OF HASTINGS

On the morning of October 14th, 1066, chill winds swept up from the sea. William stood before his men, exhorting them before the battle. He was magnificently arrayed in gleaming armor. His generals stood around him, their lances decked with banners and bright ribbons. Close by a sleek fiery stallion, a Spanish horse which the King had sent to William as a gift, was held by William's attendants. All eyes were on the great leader.

"Harold of England is forsworn!" his voice rang out confidently. "He has lied and deceived, he has not kept his faith. We of Norman blood have been blessed by the Pope, in that we may conquer England for England's sake!"

His booming voice rolled over the ranks and their confidence grew with every word he uttered. When they had crushed Harold, they were to have the finest lands in England for their reward. A roar of approval went up. The Normans shouted William's name.

"On to the Usurper!" the cry went up.

William's dark eyes flashed as he shouted back, "Let God's judgment fall upon him!"

"God help! God help! We avenge!" came the responding cry.

Now the two armies faced each other. Startled flights of starlings swooped over the ravines at the shouts of the men as they took up formation. Harold's ranks were somewhat depleted by deserters who feared the terrible ban of the Norman monk. But his knights were staunchly with him, their gilded mail armor and jeweled swords brilliant against the green slopes. They wore bright kirtles of silk and the finest linens beneath their armor. Around them gathered the brave and motley host of fighters that England had sent to defend her freedom.

William's army marched toward the battle scene with grave faces. News had come that hundreds of English ships were about to swoop down upon their fleet. They gazed off toward the horizon where Normandy lay waiting them. Few of them sang as they marched. The autumn dawn held a chill that numbed their voices and their tongues.

At the hour when William chose to attack, he had drawn his men up in three divisions. His Norman fighters surrounded him in the center, under his banner of scarlet and gold, and the azure and silver-gold standard of the Sign of the Cross. Men of Brittany and Maine took the left, while on his right the French and the Flemings swung into position. The Norman archers were placed in an advanced position before the whole host, backed by men heavily armed with mace and sword.

Harold had chosen his position well. In a nest of hills and ravines, with an occasional stream rolling through, was a level ledge which commanded all approaches to the summit and cut off the road to London. It was strategically strong because it was protected on both flanks by natural obstacles. The ledge was large enough to contain the whole Saxon army. Here Harold assembled his forces.

All through the night which preceded the battle, the Saxons labored to fortify their position. Along the open ground rose wattled barricades, strong enough to check a cavalry charge, behind which the English battle-axe could be used to deadly effect. Where no barricades had been raised, the soldiers of Harold locked their shields to serve as a wall. Behind the interlocking shields stood the Thingmen, Harold's picked guards, fierce of eye, strong of arm and determined to fight to the death.

Harold passed word along the line that under no circumstances were his forces to attack. Even if the Norman ranks broke, even if they retreated in disorder, there must be no pursuit. "Stand fast!" was the order. "Hold your ground. They cannot break through as long as we maintain our position." Harold knew that his poorly armed levies would have no chance in the open against the steel-clad Normans.

A new battle cry echoed from the English ranks. "No Normans!" cried the defenders of Hastings. "No Normans! No Normans!"

From the Normans came an answering cry of *"Dieu aide! Dieu aide!"* Because of the Pope's blessing, they were certain that God was on their side.

The Norman attack had to be delivered up a sloping advance which ran along the English front before reaching the level ridge where Harold and his men stood. If the longbow had been in use at this time, the English archers would have cut the Norman horsemen to pieces. But at this time the Saxons put little reliance in the bow. They were thick-set fellows and they liked to fight with battle-axe and pike. The Norman cavalry, therefore, met with little resistance as they ascended the slope.

The Norman advance was undoubtedly a thrilling spectacle. The cavalry came first, led by Taillefer, the minstrel. This brave fellow tossed his battle-axe in the air as he rode and sang, in a voice which sounded over the hoof-beats and the clatter of arms, the *Song of Roland*.

But the English shield-wall did not waver under the onslaught of the invaders. Cries of "No Normans! No Normans!" rose in a mighty roar.

The English wall held firm against the first attack. The "iron fish" mounted on superb battle horses swept forward like a wave toward the rising ground and the English defenders. Harold's men staunchly repulsed each surging onslaught until the trumpets rang out over the valley and the Normans withdrew from the ridge.

This was the first pitched battle the Normans had fought. They were accustomed to William's strategy in fighting, and to the Norman surprise attack. The shield-wall, this unwavering fortress of men, was different from anything they had encountered.

Again William ordered the charge, exhorting his

men and challenging them by his own daring and strength.

Taillefer's voice had been silenced almost immediately and hundreds of Normans had fallen beside him, so this second attack was made over the bodies of the fallen and wounded piled up before the shield-wall. A great wave of madly plunging horsemen charged the wall only to be beaten back. The mail-clad warriors wheeled their horses and withdrew again at the call of the trumpets

By now it was high noon and the hearts of the Normans were filled with fear. It seemed that the Standard of the Fighting Man floated above a superhuman wedge. The roaring noise of steel against steel and the English shouts had died out; silence as heavy as a shroud was broken only by the cries of the wounded.

Again the clarions rang out and the horsemen charged the English ranks a third time. Still the line held. The English axmen fought with their left hands so that the shields of the invaders were of no protection. The ground under them was slippery with the blood of both Norman and English. The

whole valley was strewn with fallen and wounded men and horses.

"The Duke is dead! The Duke is dead!"

Suddenly the air was filled with the alarming cry that the Norman leader had fallen. Confusion sent the ranks into headlong flight. In their frenzy the men of Brittany rode into the fleeing foot men. The turn in the battle had come. Forgetting the stern command of their leader, the English came pouring out from behind their wattled defenses, intent on driving the Normans down the declining ground.

William saw that his chance had come at last. He allowed his men to continue their flight until the undisciplined and poorly armed Saxons were well out in the open. Then the Norman Duke's sharp command brought the retreat to a sudden halt. The horsemen wheeled and rode like a thunderbolt into the pursuing English.

Few of the foot soldiers who had yielded to the impetus to charge down the hill returned to the position on the brow. Harold had to extend his lines hastily to fill the open gaps on his flank, and from that moment on he fought at a disadvantage. Even then he might have held his position until nightfall—and that would have meant victory—if the sagacious Norman leader had not seen a way of employing his archers to better effect. He studied Harold's still unbroken line.

"Captain of my cross-bowmen!" William shouted. "See that your men shoot their arrows in the air. Let them fall like rain."

Now the evening which was slowly coming to a close was darkened by a curtain of Norman arrows, swift and deadly, rising into the air in a graceful flight that carried them over the shield-wall into the human mass behind it.

In this deadly shower, thousands of arrows pierced limbs and bodies protected only by leather jerkins and coarse cloth. The English might have held in the face of this lethal hail from the skies if the hand of fate had not intervened. One of the arrows struck the brave Harold in the eye. From the huddled ranks about him the cry rose, "The

King is dead!" Harold lay stretched on the ground, dying in agony, and life seemed to leave the defenders with his passing. Without a leader the brave men behind the shield-wall began to break. The standard of the Fighting Man went down, with no hand to raise it again. The Normans, behind their Duke, swept over the ridge.

Darkness was beginning to fall and this enabled some of the English to get away. Most of them, however, earl and thane and peasant alike, died where they had stood all day on the blood-soaked turf.

By midnight William had cleared the place where the King had fought beneath his royal Standard; and here he ordered his pavilion set up. Torches gleamed through the black of night, casting shadows upon the gold-and-silver and gleaming jewels of the captured English banners.

The man who proved himself to be stronger than Harold stood in the desolate scene of battle, staring down upon the broken body of England's King.

"I have taken England as a conqueror but I shall rule as a king!" he told his barons.

CHAPTER XV

WILLIAM ASCENDS
THE THRONE

Following the battle of Hastings, the Conqueror was in no hurry to advance on London. As he moved his armies northward, celebrating victory with great feasts and being proclaimed the King of England by Norman rites, the desperate Saxons made a hasty move to crown Edgar the Atheling as their King.

When this news was carried to the Conqueror, the great fighter replied gravely, "A king without

an army can be no more trouble than a wasp without a sting!"

England's army had been broken. Now when the Normans swept through the countryside there was no defense left.

The crafty William had made another successful move in his game. The gates of London swung open. Edgar and his Archbishop of York came to William with the invitation to ascend the throne of England. On Christmas day, the Norman Duke took the coronation oath in Westminster Abbey. His gilded coronet was put aside forever and at last he was wearing a crown.

That night, before the clock struck midnight ending the festival of Christmas, William sat musing in his chamber. Those of his closest barons who still lived were there with him. This shrewd campaigner was forming in his mind his next move, now that he was king, so that he would become a really great sovereign.

"I have conquered," he said, pacing the floor in the smoky light of the torches, "but I come as the rightful successor to Edward. I have taken England from an arch robber who was responsible for the need to fight!" He stopped and raised his massive fist in the air. "What befalls men who are rebels? They must be treated as traitors!"

"It is the holy truth, sire King!"

William's next words brought even more pleasure to the barons. "And traitors must be made to give up their lands and their wealth to those who fought to save them!"

He swung around, facing the Norman knights. "You, by God Almighty, will become my earls, and build Norman castles where robbers and rebels once ruled!"

So it was ordered that every man who fought with Harold should give up his land and wealth to the crown of England. Many of the noblemen had died beneath the standard of the Fighting Man. There was scarcely a Saxon of noble birth who was not classed as a rebel, for England had rallied as a man to fight with Harold.

Ruthlessly and lavishly, William handed out the spoils of land and treasures to his Norman followers. One nobleman received fifty-five manors. In town another claimed sixty-eight houses. William kept for himself a generous supply of fifteen hundred English manors throughout the country.

These manors so lavishly handed out were scattered through England. The cunning William was wise enough not to let his lords become too powerful and he did not allow them to consolidate their holdings. Not only did the nobility receive rewards of beautiful English land but lowly men found themselves squires of rich estates. Norman castles sprang up all over England. A peaceful green field suddenly became a hostile place with its tower of stone and threat of power. Hills that once added only to the beauty of the landscape were transformed into bristling fortresses.

The Saxons were brave and they refused to lay down their arms. A war can be won by a single great victory but it takes more to subdue a nation. The battle of Hastings won for William the crown of England; but England itself was still an armed camp, full of islands of resistance which had to be wiped out. For a space of four years William marched and counter-marched across the face of the island

kingdom, winning local battles, storming armed towns and subduing castles.

The four years were filled with the bitterest kind of fighting and William resorted to mass slaughter in his efforts to bring the struggle to an end. The desperate English struck back. Norman soldiers were found with knives in their backs. They were waylaid in forests and on lonely roads. Small groups of Norman soldiers fell into ambushes and were wiped out. The result was that the Norman who dared to venture out alone was counted either a hero or a fool.

William passed a law stating that the murderer of a Norman had to be produced within eight days of the death or the men of the district would have to pay a heavy fine. The Saxons retaliated by mutilating the bodies beyond description. The enraged King proclaimed that *every* murdered man was of Norman birth unless the people could prove him to be a native. Four relatives had to appear before the authorities to swear to the identity. Saxons groaned under this cruel law that lasted many centuries.

Malcolm of Scotland eventually came and knelt before William, placing his hands within the King's as a pledge of his loyalty. Powerful castles rose out of the lowland country so that the frontier of Scotland was reminded that Norman barons, liegemen of William, were now the earls of the north.

William, sixth in line from Rollo, the pirate King, was at last a conqueror.

CHAPTER XVI

HEREWARD THE WAKE

William's strongest opponent did not rise against him for almost four years. In the northern confines of that part of England known as East Anglia was the fen country, a great stretch of boggy land which had no roads or bridges. It was ideal for the kind of fighting known today as guerrilla warfare. This most steadfast opponent of the conquest retreated into the very heart of the fen country, and there he kept the flag of England flying.

His name was Hereward and he is generally called "The Wake," which means The Watchful One. He was a brilliant and bold man, a small landholder who had been abroad at the time of Hastings but who came back to his native land in the hour of need. Because of the defense he maintained against the hitherto irresistible Normans, his name has come down in song and story with that of Robin Hood.

Hereward established himself on the Island of Ely, in the very heart of the fen country. He announced his intention to fight on by sending fragments of the war arrow to all parts of the country, even as far away as Wales. The sending of the war arrow was an invitation to able-bodied men who still possessed the will to fight to join up. Other races had different ways of accomplishing the same purpose. Sometimes it was done by passing of tokens, a fragment of a coin, a metal decoration. An Indian brave who got the urge to go out on the warpath would sink his tomahawk in the war post in his native village; and any others who wanted to go along would announce their intention in the same way. The war arrow of Hereward the Wake brought volunteers from all parts of England, bold men who preferred death to slavery under Norman rule.

Hereward was a great fighter. He dared to defy William and held out against him for five years. The chroniclers of those times tell us that Hereward was a soldier of such might that he was even greater than William, Harold, or Hardrada on the battle-field.

Even when he was a boy, Hereward dared to do things that called for a man's strength and courage. People talked about his feats as a rider and hunter. They liked to tell about the time he matched his strength against a huge white bear. This animal was so powerful and vicious that not even the bravest man dared to face it, choosing instead to bait other animals that were kept for this bloodthirsty amuse-ment.

The bear belonged to Gilbert of Ghent and even though Hereward begged to be allowed to fight the bear, Gilbert refused.

One day Hereward had been out hunting. He rode into Gilbert's park just in time to see the escaped bear rushing toward a small child, its long neck swaying to and fro savagely. Hereward leapt from his horse, shouting at the animal to attract its attention from the child. The bear charged Hereward. Two paces away it reared on its huge hind legs, ready to bring down its crushing forelegs upon him. He poised, sword in hand. There was only one daring thrust he could make—into the vital muzzle of the bear. He plunged at the towering body and his sword buried itself in the snout. The bear fell to the ground, yanking the sword from Hereward's hands.

That was the favorite anecdote of his youthful days. When he returned to England, he was at the peak of his power and he had won a great reputation in many Continental wars. He brought with him three things: the will to keep the struggle going, a great sword which he called Brain-biter (it was the custom of the day to find names for favorite weapons), and a beautiful wife named Torfrida. He took all three with him to the Island of Ely and there established himself in a hall which became justly famous.

The sending of the arrow had brought Hereward scores of recruits, the fen country gave him seemingly inexhaustible supplies of food, and the fens served as a barricade stronger than all the masonry in the world. Ely (which got its name originally from the prevalence of eels in the water thereabouts) was so isolated that it could be reached only by long, slim-nosed boats somewhat on the order of the North American canoe. The natives, however, preferred to do their traveling with what they called leaping poles. The fen men were so expert with these poles that they could cross a thirty-foot channel of water at one hop. The community, which boasted little more than a monastery, was on the banks of the Ouse River.

William had been convinced that the long "mopping-up" campaign, to use a modern phrase, was at an end. Then the story reached his ears of the arrival of Hereward and the sending of his war arrow. Wearily, but with savage determination, William announced that this final flurry of resistance must be wiped out instantly. He sent a small body of his men into the fen country for the purpose, but they came back convinced that Ely could not be reached. The new King of England shrugged his shoulders bitterly. "It is clear then," he said, "that I must do it myself."

He set up his first headquarters a few miles north and east of Cambridge. Here it was possible to see the spire of the monastery and the clutter of buildings which constituted the "hall" of Hereward. A quarter of a mile is a very short distance and the Conqueror was convinced that he could move his men in to attack the rebel camp without any difficulty at all.

"But, sire King," said one of the lieutenants who knew the fen country, "this is the most difficult quarter mile on the face of the earth. Know you that this mire we see will suck down a man on a horse like a twig in a stream?"

"There are no more than a handful of the stubborn dogs over there," said William. "Can we allow our authority to be flouted by this mangy band?"

"There is no way of taking armed men into Ely!" declared the lieutenant.

"What we cannot march through, we will build

a bridge around," said the King.

William had a large force with him. His men were in glittering armor and they had a great store of supplies. They were eager to get on with the conquest of Ely because of the story being circulated that the isle was filled with treasures. The volunteers who had come for a part in the defense of the last outpost of liberty had brought their possessions with them. The place, it was said, was fairly bursting with gold and jewels and precious art objects, and the King's men, being Norman, were fairly slavering to divide up the treasure. They were quite willing to take any risks.

Hereward had many brave fighters within the fortress on the Isle of Ely. They had built a heavy turf rampart around it and stockades of wooden trestles. The bog stood about it like an immense moat. Within, fifty knights sat at Hereward's table; for every knight there was a monk and they were equally prepared and armed for the fight. These defenders of Ely would gladly die for Hereward and England. They feasted together in the great hall, their tables loaded with food and their ale horns overflowing. Their minstrels sang wonderful tales of how Hereward would defy William and inspire all of England to rise up against him.

The men of Ely could look across the marches and see the sun glittering on the steel of William's soldiers who were at work preparing for the attack. On every possible occasion they slipped out among the reeds stealthily. Their soundless boats took them within range of the builders whom they harassed before speeding away into the marsh. There were great piles of stones and javelins ready inside the fort, waiting to be hurled down upon the enemy. The men watched the scurrying builders with fascination as they worked like so many ants to build a bridge over the guardian marshes. This went on for weeks and the soldiers began to grumble with impatience because Hereward would not let them strike and hurl their missiles at the Conqueror's men.

"No one will dare to strike until my trumpet rings out!" warned Hereward. "He who disobeys will pay for it. The Norman rats are building themselves a nest—let them find that it is a trap!"

William, who never failed to work out carefully

laid plans of strategy in battle, had ordered his men to drive piles into the Ouse River. But the piles would not hold. A floating bridge was then made, supported by inflated cattle hides. A huge floating sow was pushed before them as the soldiers made their way foot by foot across the slimy peat and mud. A "sow" was a strong covering used to screen the advance of attacking forces or the building of any kind of apparatus used in siege. Finally all was in readiness and a long line of the army began to advance over the causeway to the sow.

"When we march back," the King's men boasted, "we'll carry out gold and silver by the bag, like so much grain! Every man will go home with a prince's prize!"

The thought of plunder so drove the men on that soon the causeway became crowded. In the mass of men and steel, the wooden floor beneath began to sag and tilt. Knights in heavy mail slid into the mire dragging others less heavily laden with them. No one stopped to help those who sank. Their desperate cries were lost in the din of the attack.

"Drive on, Normans—let the traitors learn of

England's power!" came the booming voice of the Conqueror as they advanced.

But the on-pressing army was too great a weight for the sow. It began to slide, spilling men into the marsh like so many match sticks until all was in disorder. Those in the rear fought to save their lives; those in the front ranks were close enough to Ely to struggle on with the attack, dragging their

scaling ladders forward. Two huge drawbridges opened for them. The sow was so close to the barricade of Ely that Hereward's men could almost touch it with a pole. However, there were several yards of deep bog through which William's soldiers had to pass. With the crush from the rear, the advance ranks fell into this moat, laden with ladders, axes and spears. Their cries rose like a prolonged scream and were drowned out in the victory shouts from Ely.

Above the dreaded battle cry of the Normans and the shrieks of suffocating troops who struggled in the bog came the clear blast of Hereward's trumpets. Now a shower of arrows, stones, javelins and clubs began to rain down upon the Normans. Men who managed to reach the fortress of Ely with their ladders were hewn down by Hereward's mighty sword. Behind them the bridge began to sway under its burden of men and armor.

Norman trumpets rang out with the order to retire, and the great mass of struggling men and arms turned their backs on the island. A King and his army had been repulsed by the men of Ely.

That night there was feasting in Ely. William and his army had withdrawn to Brandon nearby. The rebels with their arch-ally, the bog, had won their first triumph. Imprisoned though the defenders were, they had no fear of William's cunning strategy. Their island was a treasure store of food. The marshes were thick with wild fowl; hundreds of ducks could be seen rising from a single mere, enough food for many a day. The streams were black with pike and eels and perch. Countless deer roamed the park lands of the isle. The swine and cattle that dotted the islands within their territory would keep the inhabitants in meat. If they needed clothing, otter and weasel and ermine could easily be sewn into jerkins and capes by the women of Ely.

However, as the days and weeks wore on into months and William's army attacked and then withdrew for stronger means of bridging the river and marshes, Hereward grew troubled in spite of the optimism among his men. He knew William to be a wily campaigner. The suspense and imprisonment was beginning to tell upon the men and women within the isle. One night Hereward talked to his wife Torfrida, who was his confidante and who often advised him wisely.

"There is only one thing to do—I will go to William's camp and learn of his plans," he told her. "Then we shall be able to build a defense that all the Norman oaths and strength cannot break through!"

Torfrida begged him not to take this risk, to let

someone else carry out his daring plan. But Hereward was determined. He set out in the ragged clothes of a wandering tradesman with some miserable wares on his back. His hair was shorn and his body darkened until he looked the part of a filthy vagrant. Hunched over and assuming a stupid expression, he managed to make his way right into the kitchen of William's court.

In this breath-taking experience he learned of William's plan of attack. He came close to losing his life, however, when he was forced into a fight with one of William's stewards. Hereward found himself dragged before William but luckily his identity was not discovered. The Conqueror spared his life but ordered him to be put in fetters for his crime. Hereward overpowered his guard and raced away to freedom.

This was what Hereward had learned: William was building a new and mighty bridge to cross the marshes, surmounted with a tower. He was enlisting a new power to help his cause, an evil witch of the district who was to mount the tower and hurl spells and incantations upon the Isle of Ely.

This evil threat troubled the leader of Ely. When he confided his story to Torfrida she begged him not to fight evil in any way except by prayer. And then she swore to lead the people of Ely by calling upon the saints; and to wear sackcloth and fetters until the Normans were driven off.

It was Torfrida who gave Hereward the idea of how this might be accomplished in spite of the witches, the strong bridge and the masses of soldiers who had been called out for the attack.

When all was in readiness for William's army, the King gazed upon the powerful structure of the bridge and its tower in front. "There stands a path that will lead us straight into the great hall of Ely!" he said confidently.

The witch was perched up on top of the tower in her flowing black robes, and her shrill voice was caught up in the breeze from the marshes as she hurled weird and terrible threats down upon Ely. The King's trumpets rang out to draw fire from the ballistas and catapults that William had brought forward. Thousands of men came along the causeway, while small boats of every type pushed out into the soggy waters of the marsh. The great attack was on!

The witch screamed and jabbered as the army moved forward. Inside the fort of Ely, men stood watching the scene in fascination. It was as if the whole of England were moving against them. Men crossed themselves as the witch's words drifted over to them. Torfrida stood before all in sackcloth and fetters, singing in a wild and excited voice.

With the oncoming rush of men and weapons, the brave men of Ely paled and steeled themselves against cold fear and panic. But their leader had promised them he was ready for William and his attack in a way which no human army could stand. As the King's men came on with a thundering roar of *"Dieu aide,"* Hereward raised his sword and gave the order, "Fire the reeds!"

Little puffs of smoke broke out all along the island. The wind picked them up and swirled them into a great cloud. Fiery hands leapt out to denser reeds and soon a mighty furnace roared between the rebels and William's army. It licked up the bridge and tower with its screaming human cargo.

The army fell back in terror and panic. Once more the bog claimed its hundreds of victims. The flames swept the full length of the marshes, devouring men in the boats and on foot.

Again William's clarions rang out the retreat. The wounded and scorched army stumbled to dry land and safety.

Hereward the Wake and his men held out against the King for five years. But the rebels had paid a price for their fatal defense of Ely. The ravage of fire had swept the reeds and marshes of fowl and wild life. Their treasure store of food was dwindling. William, in the end, was to be the victor over this brave warrior and his loyal Saxons. Ely fell. The whole island was plundered and burned. Every man was slain or taken prisoner, with the exception of a few who escaped through the marshes with Hereward who once more became an outlaw.

This last defiant stand left William a conqueror. Banners with the leopards of the Normans could be seen waving over every part of England.

CHAPTER XVII

DUTIES OF A KING

A king in those days lived with less comfort than,
say, a tenant in a cold-water walk-up apartment today. Although the castles were huge affairs, they
had been built for purposes of defense and the mere
matter of comfort never entered into the plans. In
the first place, the windows, which were narrow
slits in the thick walls, had no glass. At night or in
the case of storms, and of course all through the
winters, they were covered with wooden shutters.

The shutters did not prevent the winds or the rain or the snow from getting in but they did succeed in keeping the smoke of the open fireplaces from getting out. The Great Halls, where everyone sat down together to eat, were imposing enough but they were for show and nothing else. The food had to be brought great distances from the kitchens, which were generally in buildings outside; and everything was cold, instead of piping hot. Later the Crusades would introduce a closer trade with the East and spices would get into European countries, but at this time the meals served were not very tasty. The bedchambers were, for the most part, small niches in the thick stone walls, allowing neither light nor ventilation. If a man wanted a bath (but, of course, he seldom did), the water had to be heated in a subterranean cavern deep in the cellars, not far from the cells where prisoners were kept.

William had seen the need of a royal residence in London and had set a monk named Gundulf, who was also an architect, to raising a huge and square structure called the White Tower, around which the Tower of London is now built. Gundulf, who was called the Weeper because he had a weakness of the eyes which caused tears to run down his cheeks, would have had plenty of reason to weep if he had lived in the White Tower himself. He seems to have forgotten that people have to move about; at any rate, he equipped the building with only one narrow door. Inside there was a single stairway which had been cut out of the stone wall.

The Tower, as it happened, was a perfect hive of activity. The state prisons were in the damp cellars. William did not keep them full but there had to be, of course, turnkeys and official torturers and executioners. The King's guards occupied one floor. Above them were the Mint, the Jewel House, the Wardrobe, the Council Chamber and the Lesser Hall of the Justiciars, and all the officers, great and small, who served in these various departments. When the king was in residence, there were the nobles who held special court posts, and *their* people, the maidservants and the menservants, the grooms of the chamber and grooms of the ewery, not to mention the lackeys, the wenches, the knaves and the varlets of all degrees who had to be accommodated. It is easy to see that one dark, winding stairway and one narrow door (it was so small that only one person could enter or leave at a time) were hopelessly inadequate.

William, fortunately, did not have as large a household as later kings. Queen Matilda preferred to live in Normandy (probably after one look at that beehive of a Tower) and the royal sons were away most of the time. The Conqueror had modest tastes. He had a chief butler, a chief steward or "staller," a chamberlain and a constable.

It was perhaps not strange that the King seemed to be away from London a great deal. When he was in the West, he held court in Winchester, the old capital where the royal treasure was kept. Of the castles and manors which had been taken away from the Saxons, he had kept so many for himself that he could always sleep under his own roof no matter when nightfall might catch him. If he had to go to the turbulent North, it was invariably on military matters and then he slept in his tent.

The duties of a king were many and, for the

most part, they were difficult. It must not be supposed that once a man had a crown placed on his head he could consider himself free from all cares and above all criticism. It is closer to the truth to say that he held his post as the representative of the ruling class. The country was always divided up, in the good old days, into great tracts of land belonging to princes and dukes and earls and just plain barons. These landholders were tough individuals, determined that nothing should be allowed to interfere with *their* wealth, *their* power and *their* privileges. If a king began to do things which threatened the safety of this whole noble order, such as granting some privileges to common people, or spending some of the crown income on hospitals and schools, the landholders would get together and depose him in no time at all. Palace revolutions have come about oftener because a king wanted to do good than because he was despotic or cruel.

William, of course, ruled the land with a rod of iron and so had relatively little of this sort of thing to contend with; but if he had not been a strong man, he would have been in hot water all the time. In order to keep the conquered English in submission, he had to grant wide feudal powers to his nobles. They were allowed to build tall and strong castles at all strategic points, to keep armed forces about them and to maintain order in their own districts. Because of the obstreperous behavior of the Welsh people in the West and the Scots in the North, he established an order called Marcher Barons. These men were given land in the border sections with the understanding that they would assume the responsibility of repelling the forays of the Welsh and Scots. Needless to state, these marcher barons became a problem themselves. They ruled so completely in the lands they were protecting that the people living there had more need of protection from them than from the raiders.

Now William was long-headed and he was always full of ideas. He perceived how powerful these unscrupulous barons were becoming and he thought of a plan to pare their claws, so to speak. He kept their holding of lands broken up. A man might own a great deal of land but some of it would be near London, some in the far north, some over beside the North Sea and some in the Welsh foothills. His castles were scattered to the four corners. If he wanted to set himself up against the royal authority or enter into a baronial conspiracy, he could not get his forces all together without letting the whole kingdom know what he was trying to do. Once this wily scheme had been developed, it was practically impossible for the nobility to hatch a conspiracy. A very clever man, William; and yet he had to be very watchful of these slavering beasts of prey who were called noblemen.

Then the king had all the business of justice in his hands. The machinery of law and order in England before the Conquest had not been very effective nor had it been fair but it broke down completely after the Normans came. The barons were quite willing to take it over themselves, and to imprison and torture men and even to mutilate and hang them if they saw fit. Not wanting to allow them all this power, William had to assume the work himself. Wherever he went, he was besieged with petitions and forced to sit in judgment on lawsuits. Much of his time was spent that way. Although he proved himself a fair though ruthless judge, he much preferred the other side of the shield of kingship—the command of soldiers in the field, the conduct of diplomacy, the wider aspect generally.

Then, also, there was the matter of wardships; although no king was ever known to rebel at this particular duty. If a man of property died without heirs or with children under age, the management of the estate fell into the hands of the Court of Chancery, which meant in reality the king. This was most profitable, for the revenue could be diverted into the royal treasury and, if the king happened to be short of funds, he could sell off the livestock and cut the wood, and pocket all of the profits himself. When the heirs grew old enough to marry, the king would sell them off to the highest bidder. If it happened to be a rich heiress who was to be married off (and particularly if she happened to be pleasingly plump and passing fair) the bidding for her hand would be strenuous.

It may be of interest to explain that when the Conqueror died and was succeeded by his son William Rufus, that bloated young man tried to establish the theory that all property actually belonged to the crown and that no one could have anything more than a lease; so that, when a man died, his heirs had to buy their home and their land back from the king. The career of this avaricious individual was brought to an end by a mysterious arrow before he could get very far with his plans.

Fortunately, in later centuries, this right of wardship was taken away from the monarchs; with great difficulty, it may be said, for the kings and the chancery officers fought bitterly to prevent the loss of this choice privilege.

So, all in all, kings were very busy; and none was ever busier than William the Conqueror, who had to rebuild a nation on the ashes of a war of conquest and extermination.

CHAPTER XVIII

THE LAST YEARS

William was not only a great warrior and an able ruler but he was far ahead of the times in which he lived. As he grew older, toward the close of his reign, he proved himself a genius.

Nineteen years after the battle of Hastings, he called a midwinter assembly of the Great Council to be held at Gloucester. There was something troubling the old King by this time—he was not really too old in years but he had grown fat and slow in all his movements. William was concerned about the conditions in England brought about by so many wars.

"By the splendor of God," he exclaimed in his speech to the assembly, "we must learn more about England! We know little or nothing of this land in which we live!"

Not more than about a dozen of the noblemen present could read or write and they could scarcely conceive of the plan that was taking shape in William's mind, yet they agreed that it would help to restore order in the land if there were a written record of its valuable assets—the people and the lands possessed by them.

This was the beginning of the Domesday Book, which gives the truest picture of England in the days when the Normans cut down the Saxons with their arrows at Hastings and took England for their own. Instituting it was the most constructive and original thing that William did in the whole course of his life.

Following William's plan, England was divided into districts. Then special commissions headed by a nobleman, a bishop, and a staff of clerks started in to collect volumes of information about their districts. All up and down England, in what was to be a slow and tedious job, landowners and tenants were being questioned in detail; and records that were first checked for accuracy were being compiled. Farmers from Sussex to Northumberland were counting their cows and sheep and pigs, and reckoning up how much land they owned or worked.

All of this information was to go into a huge record, and crafty William had a very good reason for wanting it. He was genuinely interested in bringing order out of chaos throughout the country but he also realized that he had given practically all of the country away as a reward to those who had followed him in his crusade. The plan that had been forming in his mind was that these now-wealthy landowning Norman barons and loyal followers should take over the burden of what it cost to govern and defend England. But he had no way of taxing them when he did not know how much land they had or how wealthy they were.

When the Domesday Book was completed—it took several years for the commissions to cover every little village and hamlet in England—William knew how to go about raising a fortune in taxes. The trumpets of his messengers brought the people running to hear the King's proclamation. *Six shillings on each hide of land!* The first tax that William levied was on a vague measurement that was meant to represent the amount of land necessary for a free family's living requirements. Into the royal coffers rolled four hundred thousand pounds a year. Most of this was paid by Normans for they had most of the land. Now wealthy landowners raged at William as they figured out their dues to the royal mint. The Domesday Book was full of facts and figures and they had no choice but to groan and pay the price.

Matilda had been a good queen to William; so good, in fact, that when she died in 1083 he mourned her most sincerely during the four years left to him. They had a large family, including four sons and five or six (the records are not very complete on this point) daughters.

The first son was Robert who was called Curt-hose because his legs were short and fat. Poor Curt-hose was an amiable fellow and his mother's favorite but he never did find much favor in his father's eyes. The Conqueror wanted to be proud of his sons. Robert was a stout fighting man and did well in the First Crusade but he had no capacity for administration. William understood this and de-cided early that this first-born would not do to suc-ceed him as King of England. Instead he made him Duke of Normandy, a deprivation which offended Master Robert very much. After the death of the Conqueror, Robert was continuously at odds with his abler and tougher brothers and because of this he came to a very sad end.

The second son, Richard, was killed as a youth while hunting and so played no part in history.

The third son was named William. He succeeded his father on the throne and is best known in his-tory as William Rufus, because of his red hair and high complexion. He was able enough in his way but he seems to have inherited the worst traits of his father and none of the best. His end was a violent one. While out hunting with a companion he was killed by an arrow. Historians have not been able to assemble much evidence about the case and it has never been decided whether it was an accident or murder.

The fourth son was a handsome youth who became king as Henry I after the death of his red-headed and violent-tempered brother, William Rufus.

When William was sixty years old he had grown so stout that people joked about him behind his back. At this time he and Philip of France were disputing the ownership of a town on the Seine River. William was in Normandy taking cures and medicines which he hoped would make him lose weight. When word reached his ears that Philip had jested publicly about his size, he swore the oath that was so often heard on his lips: "By the splendor and resurrection of God—I'll go to Philip's land for my churching and over a hundred thousand candles there shall be the glint of steel!" His rage as he leapt from his couch was terrible to see; and when William was angered, someone always paid. Philip of France was safely beyond William's vengeance however, and so innocent persons had to suffer for his indiscreet joke and for the quarrel over the town of Nantes.

Now the whole town was to suffer. While the people were gathering their crops in, singing happily at their work, William's mounted soldiers galloped over the land setting fire to the fields.

Fruit trees and grapevines were ripped from the soil or cut down; even the beautiful shade trees were destroyed. William's rage was deep and violent and he was not satisfied until the whole town was a roaring mass of flames.

As William's horse carried him through the fire-swept area, it tripped on a burning plank and both horse and rider fell. William was injured by this fall and for six weeks he lay dying in a monastery under the walls of Rouen. It was surely divine justice that William should sustain fatal injuries in this last act of willful violence and cruelty.

The Conqueror grew weaker and weaker as the weeks passed by. He had suffered greatly and he knew that he was going to die. One day he called his favorite son, William, to his bedside. The dying King had some last words to say by way of a will.

"I cannot bequeath my kingdom to anyone," he said as he gasped for breath, "for it was not bequeathed to me. I took it by force and at the cost of blood. My wish is that my son William may obtain it if he please God. Thus I leave it in God's hands."

As these last few words of the great warrior and conquering King were whispered, he was acknowledging the truth that he had taken a crown by force, one to which he had had no rights.

However, there was to be new blood in England. Two races were to be welded together. This transfusion was to be the beginning of a great empire. The vigorous Normans, the men who set out from the Northland with the adventuresome Rollo, were to mix their blood with the blood of the Saxons.

The boy Duke who became a conqueror and later was called William the Great had maneuvered his plan for power with all the genius of a warrior-statesman. It might be said that he was a pawn in a far greater game than the one he so shrewdly played for a crown.

INDEX

Index

Index